LORD JIM: CENTENNIAL ESSAYS

Edited by Allan H. Simmons and J. H. Stape

Amsterdam - Atlanta, GA 2000

To the memory of Ian Watt

1917-1999

scholar and friend

Contents

Foreword	vii
Notes on Contributors	ix
Lord Jim and Embarrassment MICHAEL GREANEY	1
Bakhtin's Monologism and the Endings of *Crime and Punishment* and *Lord Jim* CEDRIC WATTS	15
"He was misleading": Frustrated Gestures in *Lord Jim* ALLAN H. SIMMONS	31
Reading as Homecoming: Expatriation as a Critical Discourse in *Lord Jim* LUDMILLA VOITKOVSKA	48
"Usque ad Finem": *Under Western Eyes*, *Lord Jim*, and Conrad's Red Uncle ANDRZEJ BUSZA	64
Louis Becke's Gentlemen Pirates and *Lord Jim* J. H. STAPE	72
The Missing Crew of the *Patna* GENE M. MOORE	83
John Dos Passos on *Lord Jim* ROBERT W. TROGDON	99
Newspaper Accounts of the *Jeddah* Affair GENE M. MOORE, COMPILER	104

Foreword

Writing to Philippe Neel on 24 October 1922 to thank him for his translation of *Lord Jim* Conrad allowed himself a rare and, if we may make bold to judge, a proper moment of self-congratulation. Confessing that he had not read the novel for some time, he reported to his translator some of his responses while he was re-reading it: "Et je me disais: 'Ah, c'est très bien ça! ... Tiens c'est remarquable.' ... 'Quelle belle langue' et ainsi de suite, d'exclamation en exclamation d'étonnement et de plaisir." [And I said to myself: '*That* is good! ... That is remarkable...' 'How well written!' and so on, going from exclamation to exclamation of astonish-ment and pleasure.] (*Lettres françaises* 176).

A hundred years after the novel's original publication, it seems appropriate to recall its creator's emotions, those shared now by generations of readers, both of the "common" and scholarly kind. How good, and remarkable, and well written, it is indeed. Those might be reasons enough to mark the centenary of its publication and celebrate its continuing popularity. The hundred-year mark that promises enduring interest has now been reached, and the novel has certainly survived, having been subjected to critical approaches that have come and gone, from its contemporary belletristic reception to New Criticism to archetypal criticism and Freudian analysis. During the Second World War a Polish translation had a special vogue, offering what was thought to be a vision of fidelity and heroism at a time of extreme crisis. In the 1960s an appallingly bad film was made of it. A bar in one of Bangkok's best five-star hotels (where Conrad assuredly never stayed) sports its name today. A new generation of feminist and post-colonialist critics have interrogated the text from perspectives that have shed new light, and not a little heat, and the full weight of "theory" and the culture wars have been brought to bear on it. *Lord Jim* continues to be reprinted and translated, and remains a cornerstone in Conrad's canon, the achievement by which he is often enough popularly known.

The centenary of its publication offers no occasion to attempt a facile summing up, a futile task given that the novel's protean capacities; its sheer thematic amplitude and variety, assure that any view of it will always be partial. The outpouring of articles and chapters of books and even whole books demonstrate the novel's Everest-like position in the Conrad canon and in literary Modernism generally. What is attempted here is more modest and, we hope, useful. If *Lord Jim* cannot be "seen whole," that laudable but, as we now think, impossible Arnoldian aim, the various scholars whose work appears here have nonetheless attempted to see various aspects of it "steadily."

In putting together the present group of essays on this perennially changing and challenging text we have deliberately aimed to offer both criticism and scholarship, to not out that old if admittedly leaky distinction. The present collection thus takes into its purview new information about the novel's sources and reception as well as readings that focus on its thematics, its narrative strategies, and the play and interplay of its meanings. Like its title-character, there is an essential elusiveness about the novel that promises always to make it a ground for continuing debate and enquiry from myriad viewpoints.

The essays here are, then, in one sense, a "take" on *Lord Jim* at this moment in time, necessarily reflecting currently available critical approaches, but they also look forward, suggesting directions that might be fruitfully pursued. And there are, happily, many things yet to do. For one, serious textual analysis is still in its infancy, and in the coming years the text of the novel read for the past hundred will undergo recension and cleaning. The search for its sources, begun by John D. Gordan in the 1940s, as some of the work here shows, has not come to an end even if, thanks to the research of Norman Sherry and Hans van Marle, the novel's main real-life quarries are known. Whatever the shifts to come in criticism, it is difficult to see *Lord Jim* being shunted to the side. Its place in the history of the Modernism seems secure, and as Conrad himself would have it, it is simply "remarkable."

Allan H. Simmons
J. H. Stape

NOTES ON CONTRIBUTORS

ANDRZEJ BUSZA, a poet, translator, and Conrad scholar, is Associate Professor in the Department of English and the Programme in Comparative Literature at the University of British Columbia. His publications include *Conrad's Polish Literary Background*, an edition of *The Rover* with J. H. Stape, and most recently an essay on Conrad and the Moderns in a special issue of the *Stanford Humanities Review* devoted to the career of Ian Watt.

MICHAEL GREANEY is a Lecturer in English Literature at Lancaster University. He is currently completing a book entitled *Conrad's Storytellers*, on linguistic communities and narrative methods in Conrad's major fiction.

GENE M. MOORE is a Lecturer in English at the University of Amsterdam. The author of *Proust and Musil: The Novel as Research Instrument* (1985) and editor of *Conrad's Cities* (1992) and *Conrad on Film* (1997), he has recently co-authored *The Oxford Reader's Companion to Conrad* (2000) and is currently co-editing *Suspense* for the Cambridge Edition of the Works of Joseph Conrad.

ALLAN H. SIMMONS is a Senior Lecturer in the English Department at St. Mary's College, Strawberry Hill. He has published widely on the work of Joseph Conrad. His recent publications include the Centennial Edition of *The Nigger of the "Narcissus"* for Everyman and contributions to *The Oxford Reader's Companion to Conrad*.

J. H. STAPE has taught at universities in Canada, France, and the Far East. His recent publications include a critical edition of Virginia Woolf's *Orlando* (1998) and contributions to *The Oxford Reader's Companion*s to Hardy and to Conrad. He is co-editing *Lord Jim* for the Cambridge Edition of the Works of Joseph Conrad.

ROBERT W. TROGDON is Assistant Professor of English at Kent State University and Assistant Executive Director of the Cambridge Edition of Joseph Conrad. He is the editor of *Ernest Hemingway: A Documentary Volume* (1999) and author of various articles on Hemingway.

LUDMILLA VOITKOVSKA is Assistant Professor of Comparative Literature and Slavic Studies at the University of Saskatchewan, and has published on cultural studies, translation, and linguistics. She is presently working on a book entitled *The Generic Structure of The Expatriate Novel in Conrad and Nabokov*.

CEDRIC WATTS is Professor of English at Sussex University. His biographical and critical books on Conrad include *The Deceptive Text: An Introduction to Covert Plots* (1984), *Joseph Conrad: A Literary Life* (1989), *Joseph Conrad: "Nostromo"* (1990), and *A Preface to Conrad* (2nd edition, 1993).

NOTE ON CITATIONS

All citations from the works of Joseph Conrad are from Dent's Collected Edition (London: J. M. Dent and Sons, 1946-55). Unless otherwise stated, letters are cited from *The Collected Letters of Joseph Conrad*, edited by Frederick R. Karl and Laurence Davies (Cambridge: Cambridge University Press, 1983 onwards), abbreviated as: *CL*. For ellipses, the use of three spaced points indicates an ellipsis in the original text and three unspaced points indicates an ellipsis introduced by the contributor.

LORD JIM AND EMBARRASSMENT

Michael Greaney
Lancaster University

"I wanted to see him squirm," says Charlie Marlow, when he recalls catching sight of Jim for the first time just as news of the *Patna* scandal was breaking. Jim's apparent nonchalance, his "don't-care-hang air" (46), prompts this punitive fantasy on the part of his future mentor; but Marlow soon learns that, far from being immune to shame, Jim is an incurably embarrassment-prone figure whose unhappy knack of exposing himself to public humiliation will come to occupy a significant portion of his life-story. And not only Jim will have reason to squirm in this text. Like a blush spreading guiltily across the body, his shame radiates out to encompass an entire community of European sailors and expatriates – Marlow, the French Lieutenant, Captain Brierly, and many others – all of whom participate in the crisis of collective embarrassment of which *Lord Jim* is a case-study. The observation that embarrassment is contagious, that it transmits itself from the original "victim" to susceptible bystanders and spectators, is not, of course, strikingly new; but what is strikingly different and valuable about this text is the manner in which its structure has been contorted by the collective embarrassment of the *Patna* affair to such an extent that embarrassment has become part of the very experience of reading.

My claim that *Lord Jim* is one of the great novels of embarrassment in our literature is not one that receives immediate corroboration from the wealth of critical commentary on it. Embarrassment has not been ignored by *Lord Jim*'s readers, but it has on the whole been subordinated to themes of more obvious *gravitas*: ethical questions of responsibility and betrayal, existential questions ("how to be"), narratological problems of structure and point-of-view, and ideological questions over the text's affiliations to imperial discourse and capitalist ideology, have all massively overshadow the issue of embarrassment in the history of the novel's reception. But if Conrad's readers have tended to overlook the presence of embarrassment *in* the novel, it is well worth noticing that a considerable number of them have been embarrassed *by* the novel. There is much in *Lord Jim* to make the fastidious reader squirm: there is the notorious "collapse" from high seriousness to escapist fantasy; there are those tell-tale signs of the novel's origins as a short story; and there is the eccentric narrative style of "that preposterous master mariner" Charlie Marlow.¹ It would not be too difficult for an unsympathetic reader to represent *Lord Jim* as a botched masterpiece, hugely ambitious but clumsily and unevenly executed. I would not endorse such an ungenerous verdict on the novel myself, but neither do I think that its "structural embarrassments" can be ingeniously explained away. It is entirely appropriate, I think, that a novel so exquisitely sensitive to its characters' pangs of embarrassment should induce something of the same emotion in its readers. Embarrassment is a necessary and valuable, if frequently uncomfortable, part of the experience of reading *Lord Jim*.

Before I consider the novel in detail, however, I must address the question of terminology. Embarrassment is easy to recognize but not easy to define. Consult a thesaurus, and you will find "embarrassment" rubbing shoulders with half-a-dozen near-synonyms: "shame," "humiliation," "mortification," "guilt," "abashment," and "disgrace." These terms are frequently deployed in *Lord Jim* itself, in the course of Marlow's richly nuanced exploration of the subjective experience of moral failure. It might therefore seem a somewhat arbitrary decision to privilege "embarrassment" above its semantic neighbours as the master-term of this essay. As a preliminary move, then, I should sort through this cluster of interrelated (but not necessarily interchangeable) terms; and I take my cue from Marlow himself, who deplores the fact that Jim "made so much of his disgrace while it is the guilt alone that matters" (177). Speaking here with unusual severity on Jim's case, Marlow articulates a clear opposition between "disgrace" (what we might colloquially term "loss of face") and "guilt" (an inner sense of culpability or blameworthiness).

This opposition has been echoed in influential readings of *Lord Jim* by Ian Watt and John Batchelor, although they both prefer to speak of "shame" rather than "disgrace."² Working with definitions laid down by the psychologist Gerhart Piers, Watt argues for reading *Lord Jim* as a novel of shame; his argument is reinforced by Batchelor, who associates the novel with the "shame culture" phase of Greek civilization. According to Piers, the difference between guilt and shame is that the former is a

---

[1] The expression is Henry James's (see Ford, 160-61).
[2] See Watt (1980), 341-44, and Batchelor (1988), 168-69.

feeling of moral culpability, whilst the latter is a feeling of personal failure. Guilt arises from a sense of having committed a crime or infringed a law; shame arises from a sense of having publicly failed to live up to one's idealized self-image (Piers and Singer, 1971, 11). Applying Piers's definitions to Jim's case, it becomes clear that shame, not guilt, is his dominant emotion in the aftermath of the *Patna* incident. Jim is not conspicuously distressed by his breach of maritime law; nor does his betrayal of the sleeping pilgrims in his care prey on his mind; what rankles is his humiliating failure to seize the opportunity for heroism of which he had dreamed for so long. It is Jim's wounded self-esteem, rather than his guilty conscience, to which Marlow ministers during their series of painful debriefings.

But to characterize shame as nothing more than a form of narcissistic self-pity – which is what Marlow appears to do when he insists that "the guilt alone ... matters" – is unfairly dismissive. Shame in *Lord Jim* encompasses both affective experience (the "shame" of the individual) and collective experience (the rituals of punishment and exclusion whereby the individual is "shamed"). Building on the insights of Batchelor and Watt, it would be possible to read the novel not simply as a case-study in the psychology of shame, but as an exercise in comparative anthropology that juxtaposes two radically different "shame cultures": the world of the *Patna* and the world of Patusan. My own project is more modest: I shall focus on embarrassment, which I regard as a milder version of shame. Embarrassment, like shame, is a consequence of a humiliating display of personal fallibility; it arises when the coherent self one tries to project is at odds with the imperfect self one involuntarily reveals. It differs from shame on several counts: first, it is commonly understood as a relatively minor form of shame, often associated with shyness or self-consciousness; it can be a desperately uncomfortable experience, even when it arises from the most trifling *faux pas*; it is cruelly self-perpetuating – embarrassment is embarrassing, both for its victim and its audience; and it has unmistakable physical and verbal symptoms, such as blushing or stammering. To emphasize the fact that Jim's shame chiefly manifests itself in the very particular form of embarrassment is in no way to diminish the seriousness of *Lord Jim*; rather, it is a valuable way of highlighting the peculiarly tragicomic form that Jim's crisis takes.

The key precedent for taking embarrassment seriously as a literary category is Christopher Ricks's *Keats and Embarrassment*. Ricks's book is both a tribute to the exceptional tact and generosity with which Keats handles the experience of embarrassment, and an answer to those ungenerous critics who find Keats's verse to be embarrassingly twee or self-indulgent. The Keats of *Keats and Embarrassment* stands for what one might call "Romantic embarrassment": a sense of the body as the site of both the hot flush of passion and the blush of awkwardness; and a sense of the imagination's capacity to recognize and transcend such uncomfortable dualities. There are moments when Ricks's analysis is extremely suggestive of *Lord Jim*. For example, when he describes embarrassment as "a binding chain-reaction" which can be "dislinked and released by one imaginative act of sympathy" (Ricks, 43), he might almost have been referring to Marlow's sympathetic effort to release Jim from the chains of embarrassment. But on the whole Ricks's ideas are formulated in such intimate contact with Keats's writings that they cannot simply be detached from their original contexts and mechanically applied to a text belonging to a different genre and a different era. A possible route from "Romantic embarrassment" to the "Modernist embarrassment" of Conrad is offered in *Telling Complexions*, Mary Ann O'Farrell's study of the blush in nineteenth-century fiction. O'Farrell develops two conflicting theories about the blush: a "Foucauldian" argument that the blush is one of the means whereby the body is submitted to social legibility, and a "Barthesian" argument to the effect that those who blush can derive a perverse pleasure from their own bodily legibility. She pursues this dialectic through detailed readings of Jane Austen, Elizabeth Gaskell, Charles Dickens, Mary Elizabeth Braddon, Anthony Trollope, George Eliot, and Henry James. In some senses it is hardly surprising that O'Farrell can find no space for Conrad in her Great Tradition of blushing: the blush is an expression of the drawing-room, not the high seas or the wilderness. But there are tantalizing connections between James and Conrad on this matter. It is particularly interesting to recall that James published a collection of short stories entitled *Embarrassments* in 1896, just three years before instalments of *Lord Jim* began to appear in *Blackwood's Magazine*. It is unlikely that this volume – which comprises "The Figure in the Carpet," "Glasses," "The Next Time," and "The Way It Came" – provided anything in the way of direct inspiration for *Lord Jim*; but we do know that Conrad was reading James with supreme admiration in the 1890s, and it has been very plausibly suggested that the refinements in Conrad's narrative technique from *Heart of Darkness* onwards may owe something to James, so it seems reasonable to argue that the presence of embarrassment in *Lord Jim* is symptomatic of a "post-Jamesian" preoccupation with the revealing minutiae of social intercourse. Of course the influence of James did not always bring out the best in Conrad. The "lacerating embarrassment" (Watt, 1968, 302) of Conrad's fulsome letters to James is not easy to forget; and James always seemed distinctly embarrassed by "poor dear J.C."[3] At times the relationship between James, the reluctant guru, and Conrad, the wayward disciple, is oddly reminiscent of that between Marlow and Jim.

"[A] horrible bungler" (155) is one of Marlow's more exasperated descriptions of his protégé. It would possible to see Jim's entire professional and personal life as a series of gaffes and blunders, none of which is harder to live down than the *Patna* scandal. Abandoned by Jim and his fellow officers, who are convinced that it is about to sink, the *Patna*, and its human cargo of 800 Mecca-bound pilgrims, miraculously stays afloat: a potentially tragic shipwreck becomes a farcical non-shipwreck. This dereliction of duty is a victimless crime, a grotesquely embarrassing blunder that leaves the *Patna* and the pilgrims intact, but Jim's dignity in tatters. Not only has Jim squandered a golden opportunity for heroism, but he has become the laughing-stock of the entire Malay Archipelago, fleeing from one port to the next with the derisive laughter of countless sailors ringing in his ears. Jim bitterly refers to himself as the victim of a "joke hatched in hell" (108); Marlow takes up this metaphor, referring to the "practical joke" (108) and the "infernal joke" (109) of the *Patna* incident. Keats once wrote that "the most unhappy hours in our lives are those in which we recollect time past to our own blushing – If we are immortal that must be the Hell" (cited in Ricks, 21). This seems to capture the kind of hell Jim inhabits after the *Patna*; indeed, Jim is doomed not merely to recollect time past to his own blushing, but in a sense to re-enact it. Constantly embarrassing himself, and a constant source of embarrassment for others, Jim has a regrettable talent for attracting the wrong sort of attention – there is his initial confrontation with Marlow on the courthouse veranda (70-76), his hysterical laughter at the Malabar House (100), his unseemly scuffle with a "cross-eyed Dane" (199) in Schomberg's hotel. Each successive embarrassing scrape in which Jim finds himself functions as a minor recapitulation of the primary embarrassment of the *Patna*.

---

[3] Letter to Edith Wharton, 27 February 1914, in Stape and Knowles, eds., 97.

It is the farcical scandal of the *Patna* that first brings Jim to Marlow's attention; and it is an embarrassing altercation outside the courthouse that first brings the novel's two heroes together. This scene, which pivots on Jim's failure to recognise the source and referent of the phrase "wretched cur," is probably the best known instance of the Modernist technique of "symbolic deciphering" in Conrad's fiction (Watt, 1980, 273-85.) But, as Jacques Berthoud has pointed out, the scene is also "a brilliantly imagined treatment of the psychology of mortification" (1978, 81). I would suggest that this association between Modernism and mortification is by no means coincidental. The common denominator between Jim's embarrassing mistake and Conrad's innovative technique is the idea of a breakdown in communication. When Marlow and Jim confront one another – the former almost speechless with surprise, the latter fulminating incoherently and spoiling for a fight – it is as though they are speaking different languages. This encounter is exquisitely embarrassing and painfully funny; but Conrad does more than simply extract humour from the "wretched cur" incident. The interlude of miscommunication between Jim and Marlow exemplifies Conrad's characteristically Modernist sense of language as a system of slippery, equivocal signs that have to be coaxed into transparent intelligibility.

Images of crisis have a tendency to become aesthetic possibilities in Conrad's hands. Not only does the breakdown of language between Jim and Marlow usher in the sophisticated technique of "symbolic deciphering"; it also precedes what is probably the most vivid of Jim's many blushes in the novel:

> I looked at him. The red of his fair sunburnt complexion deepened suddenly under the down of his cheeks, invaded his forehead, spread to the roots of his curly hair. His ears became intensely crimson, and even the clear blue of his eyes was darkened many shades by the rush of blood to his head. His lips pouted a little, trembling as though he had been on the point of bursting into tears. I perceived he was incapable of pronouncing a word from the excess of his humiliation. (74)

Charles Darwin has described the blush as 'the most human of all expressions' (1890, 328), and it is the function of the blush to humanize Jim. Jim begins the novel longing for a "textual" identity – he wants to be "a hero in a book" (6) – but the blush is a forcible reminder of his flesh-and-blood reality. Luxuriating in self-confidence as the *Patna* glides serenely westward, Jim felt "a pleasurable languor running through every limb as though all the blood in his body had turned to warm milk" (21). This remarkable simile is suggestive of a transformation from guilt to innocence, a regression from full-blooded humanity to infantile *naiveté*; but the guilty blood will soon surge back into Jim's veins. And Jim's blush will intensify in the consciousness of his visibility. "A single word had stripped him of his discretion," Marlow remarks, "discretion which is more necessary to the decencies of our inner being than clothing is to the decorum of our body'" (74). The idea of Jim stripped bare inescapably recalls the archetypal image of shame in Western culture, that of Adam and Eve being expelled from Eden, conscious for the first time of their nakedness.

Red faces are everywhere in *Lord Jim*, but not all of them denote postlapsarian fallibility. Attending the Court of Inquiry, Marlow describes Jim's "burning cheeks" (28), refers to "the shame that made you burn" (28), and notices the "red faces" (28) of the nautical assessors. In the "intolerably stuffy" Sydney café where he encounters the French Lieutenant, Marlow's face "burned as though I had been young enough to be embarrassed and blushing" (140). And whatever else changes in Patusan, Jim still has "his old trick of stubborn blushing" (248). The red face does not always denote embarrassment: passion, anger, or the tropical sunshine are all equally plausible causal factors. The red face does not always lead us unerringly to someone's "inner being"; frequently, it functions as an ambiguous "writing of the body" that demands interpretation. In the light of one captain's remark about Jim's tendency to "blush like a girl" (195), it seems likely that sexuality and gender have a part of play in any full analysis of blushing in this text. Indeed, Tony Tanner has even described a blush as a "sort of mild erection of the head" (1972, 35). It seems likely that many of the blushes in *Lord Jim* are prompted by the excitements and embarrassments of passionate male friendship. Whether there is a sexual frisson between Marlow and Jim, or whether the text as a whole might be described as homoerotic, has been the subject of some recent critical debate.[4] Perhaps the most accurate term to describe the intimate male world of *Lord Jim* is "homosocial," a term Eve Kosofsky Sedgewick coined to describe the continuum between social and sexual experience in men-only relationships. The homosocial element in

---

[4] See Lange (1992), Harpham (1996), and Ruppel (1998).

Lord Jim manifests itself in curiously contradictory ways. For example, Marlow makes no secret of the fact that Jim is physically attractive – "his personal appearance, his hair, his eyes, his smile, made friends for him wherever he went" (198) – and he also speaks of being "captivated" by the handsome Malay chieftain Dain Waris (262). But elsewhere homosocial desire emerges in much more guarded and embarrassed ways: many of Marlow and Jim's tête-à-têtes are taken up with awkward silences, strained confidences, and fumbled handshakes. "He coloured all over," Marlow recalls of one particularly tense moment, "while in my confusion I half-choked myself with my own tongue" (154). Given that Jim and Marlow are part of a community that enforces male camaraderie but prohibits homosexuality, it is perhaps unsurprising that their relationship – which is a kind of love-story – should be prone to awkwardness and confusion. Indeed, one of the central ideological embarrassments for *Lord Jim* as a whole is that its affectionate portrait of a male-centred world should reveal desires that are anything but patriarchal.

I have already touched on the role of vision and visibility in embarrassment. An irresistible illustration of this connection is offered in Henry James's "Glasses," whose heroine, Flora Saunt, is a beautiful young woman with failing sight who would rather go blind than wear the cumbersomely ugly corrective spectacles designed for her. Flora ends the story blind but radiantly beautiful, having surrendered her eyesight to escape the wrong sort of visibility. Jim, too, feels like a prisoner of his own visibility. In the novel's early chapters, a thousand pairs of eyes seem to be fixed on him: the opening page takes the measure of him with cool irony – an inch or so below the regulation six-feet; he is the object of a punishing collective gaze in the courtroom; and Marlow's intent scrutiny on the veranda brings him into microscopic close-up. The desire to see Jim is one of the most powerful in this text, but there is an equally strong impulse in the opposite direction. Visual desire, or "wanting to see" ("I wanted to see him squirm"), is counter-balanced in this text by "wanting not-to-see." In his book on *Heart of Darkness*, Cedric Watts refers to the Accountant at the Outer Station who has developed the capacity to ignore or block out the vileness and horror that surround him. Watts calls this capacity the "ostrich-factor." The ostrich's fabled tendency to bury its head in the sand strikes me as a perfect image of wanting not-to-see, of finding a given spectacle too embarrassing or distressing to contemplate. Aboard the *Patna* Jim tries to glue his eyes shut as the tragic farce unfolds (105); but perhaps no character displays the reverse of visual desire more strongly than Captain Brierly, who buttonholes Marlow with a plan to help Jim abscond: "This infernal publicity is too shocking: there he sits while all these confounded natives, serangs, lascars, quartermasters are giving evidence that's enough to burn a man to ashes with shame" (67). Jim looks for all the world like an exemplary specimen of English imperial masculinity, but – according to Brierly – acts in a way that would shame those "natives, serangs, lascars, quartermasters," those non-European, non-officer class sailors for whom Brierly has such contempt. Jim is a colossal embarrassment to the European colonial establishment, and Brierly wants him banished from sight: "let him creep twenty feet underground and stay there! By heavens! *I* would" (66). Marlow echoes this sentiment much later – "I merely wished to achieve his disappearance" (229) – but the effort to blot Jim out of everyone's field of vision is achieved not through the schemes of Marlow and Brierly but rather at the level of narrative discourse. Throughout the novel Marlow is at pains to stress Jim's inscrutability: he is "under a cloud" (416), enveloped by mist, always tantalizingly faint and out-of-focus. His single most important action in the entire text – the jump from the *Patna* – is initially overlooked and then glimpsed in fragmentary, disorientating retrospect. Somehow, Jim manages to be all too embarrassingly visible *and* a blind-spot at the heart of this novel. If James's Flora Saunt sacrifices her vision to escape from personal embarrassment, Conrad's *Lord Jim* dispenses with the all-seeing eye of the classic realist text in order not to have to witness the full spectacle of its hero's shame.

If embarrassment tends to interfere with clarity of vision, it can also rob its victim of the power of speech. The sight of Jim on the veranda of the courtroom "incapable of pronouncing a word from the excess of his humiliation" (74) should prepare us for the dozens of occasions upon which words will fail our tongue-tied hero. Not that Jim's stumbling discourse reflects badly on him; after all, the inarticulate characters in Conrad – Singleton, Stevie – are often also the most admirable. Indeed, Conrad elevates his distrust of eloquence to an aesthetic principle in his "Preface" to *The Nigger of the "Narcissus,"* where he argues that the artist must abandon all "-isms" and be true to the "stammerings of his conscience" (xi). The stammerings of Jim's conscience are audible throughout *Lord Jim*. Nearly every passage of his dialogue contains gaps and hesitations – none more famous than in the following crestfallen confession:

"'I had jumped . . .' He checked himself, averted his gaze. . . . 'It seems'" (111). Where one might expect to see a moment-by-moment account of Jim's thought-processes, Conrad gives us instead a double aporia in the form of two aposiopetic breaks: the gap in Marlow's discourse repeats and in a sense confirms the gap in Jim's – confirms it in the sense of establishing the gap as a credible narrative strategy rather than an empty space in the text. Jim has not failed to narrate; rather, he has taken us to the limits of the narratable. His sentence is not clumsily unfinished; it fades out into eloquent silence. As so often in *Lord Jim*, one of Jim's embarrassing vices has been transformed into an aesthetic virtue.

I have suggested that one of the tasks *Lord Jim* sets itself is to "redeem" Jim from embarrassment. In displaying a certain solidarity with its hero, however, Conrad's novel has laid itself open to the charge of being an "embarrassing" text. For all its undeniable narrative virtuosity, the novel retains a certain awkwardness of construction, seen chiefly in its notorious broken-backed structure. There is also something rather clumsy and indecisive in the way the text continually announces and then postpones its own ending. What is intriguing about these structural embarrassments is the way they mirror Jim's flaws. For example, when the novel enters Patusan it appears to have forgotten all the sobering lessons of the *Patna* section. Jim's romantic dreams of heroism, which were exposed as the stuff of naive escapist fantasy in the first part of the novel, are spectacularly fulfilled in the second. Jim's exploits in Patusan – where he escapes from captivity, dispatches would-be assassins, topples the evil warlord Sherif Ali, falls in love with a beautiful girl, wins lifelong friends and loyal servants, and becomes *de facto* ruler of a flourishing province – could almost have been culled from the schoolboy adventure fiction that nourished his imagination before he went to sea. It is as though Conrad has been captivated by the very fantasies he set out to debunk; the "jump" from the world of the *Patna* to the world of Patusan is as catastrophic in its own way as Jim's jump from the *Patna*.

The "collapse" in this text from High Modernism to a relatively straightforward story of good and evil has exercised numerous critics, and I do not propose here to rehearse the entire critical debate on this issue. Instead, I simply want to point to the radically opposed positions occupied by two very different critics: F. R. Leavis and Fredric Jameson. In the substantial, and substantially sympathetic, chapter on Conrad in *The Great Tradition*, Leavis disposes of *Lord Jim* in two brisk paragraphs. The novel's first part, Leavis informs us, is "good Conrad," but "the romance that follows" – Jim's career in Patusan – is not (1948, 218). Nothing in the way of detailed evidence is produced to substantiate these judgements. Leavis does not dwell on this verdict, beyond lumping the Patusan section with *Almayer's Folly*, *An Outcast of the Islands*, and *Tales of Unrest* – works that, Leavis informs us, "aren't easy to re-read" (218). Leavis's claim that the early Malay fiction, and, by implication, the Patusan section, isn't "easy to re-read," is unfortunately symptomatic of the dismissiveness of his critical method. Those of us who associate Leavis with a Cambridge tradition of "close reading" would do well to remind ourselves that acts of non-reading are not rare in his criticism. His argument is a refusal to read masquerading as a denial of legibility. Just as Brierly wants Lord Jim banished "twenty feet underground," so Leavis wants *Lord Jim* banished from the Great Tradition into the oblivion of the unreadable.

Let me juxtapose Leavis's curt verdict on *Lord Jim* with the lengthy discussion of the novel in Jameson's *Political Unconscious*, probably the most theoretically sophisticated reading that the novel has received. Jameson's starting point (the perception that *Lord Jim* is a novel of two halves) is identical to Leavis's, but the resemblance ends there. He sees the "break" in *Lord Jim* not as a sign of authorial incompetence, but as deeply symptomatic of its place in cultural history. Written in the aftermath of the structural breakdown of nineteenth-century realism, *Lord Jim* provides a record of the cultural moment when realism was being hived off into the dialectically opposed realms of highbrow Modernism and the populist, mass-culture. Not everyone has been convinced by Jameson's interpretation of Conrad,[5] but it is nevertheless representative of a broadly "post-structuralist" fondness for ruptured, self-divided texts. The divisions in *Lord Jim* that so embarrassed Leavis have become, for the post-structuralist critic, the very condition of its exemplary readability.

The other major "structural embarrassment" of the novel is its apparent inability to come to a dignified end: Marlow is a raconteur who evidently doesn't know when, or how, to quit. His oral narrative and its epistolary supplement frequently gesture towards an impending conclusion that is then postponed or simply forgotten. It is customary to regard these "false endings" as residual evidence of *Lord Jim*'s origins as a short tale for *Blackwood's* that somehow ballooned, as successive instalments

---

[5] See especially Berthoud (1985).

appeared, into a full-length novel. Viewed in this way, *Lord Jim*'s false endings are simply irrelevant textual relics that a vigilant editor should have weeded out before the book version appeared; but my argument is that the novel's problematic (non-)endings play significantly into its general preoccupation with the delicate processes of parting, valediction, and closure – processes with which Ricks is concerned in the final chapter of his book on Keats. Writing on the "various filiations of parting to embarrassment" (211), Ricks explores Keats's tactful perceptions of the potential for awkwardness and poignancy in any leave-taking. A comparable awareness is evident in Conrad's valedictory scenes in *Lord Jim*. Consider, for example, the parting between Jim and Marlow at the end of their first meal together:

> [A]t the moment of taking leave he treated me to a ghastly muddle of dubious stammers and movements, to an awful display of hesitations. God forgive him – me! He had taken it into his fanciful head that I was likely to make some difficulty as to shaking hands. It was too awful for words. I believe I shouted suddenly at him as you would bellow to a man you saw about to walk over a cliff; I remember our voices being raised, the appearance of a miserable grin on our face, a crushing clutch on my hand, a nervous laugh. ... the thing was over at last, with a groan that floated up to me in the dark. He got himself away somehow. The night swallowed his form. He was a horrible bungler. Horrible. (155)

This bungled leave-taking initiates a whole series of awkward and poignant valedictory scenes: an uncomfortable silence descends on Marlow's conversation with the French Lieutenant as they part company (148-49), whilst Jim makes another hash of taking leave as he dithers on the threshold of Marlow's hotel room (180-81). A little over half-way through the novel, Marlow informs his audience that there remains "little to be told of Jim" (224), and announces that "My last words about Jim shall be few" (225). Prior to Jim's departure on Stein's brigantine, Marlow and Jim "clasped each other's hands and exchanged the last hurried words" (240). Some two years later another valedictory scene takes place, Jim and Marlow shaking hands at the mouth of the Patusan river for possibly the last time (334-36). Marlow will later announce in his letter to the "privileged man" that it is "through the eyes of others that we take our last look at him" (339) – a final glimpse that occupies some hundred pages. Commenting on the novel's obsession with leave-taking, Batchelor has written: "Since at least chapter 21 the novel has been hugging its valedictory gestures, reiterating its last lingering looks at Jim to a point where in the hands of any lesser craftsman they could be tedious or risible" (1994, 113). It is worth noticing the slightly defensive tone of these words. Batchelor is *almost* embarrassed by Conrad, but he is right, all the same, to read the novel as a long and painful farewell to nineteenth-century values. *Lord Jim* tests our capacity for readerly embarrassment, and it tests our capacity to see embarrassment as more than merely embarrassing. In its resistance to closure, the text displays the qualities of open-endedness and anti-finality that Bakhtin so admired in Dostoevsky. But the text does, finally, have to come to an end, bringing Jim, Stein, Marlow, and the butterflies together in a multiple leave-taking from which any sense of embarrassment is poignantly absent:

> He is gone, inscrutable at heart, and the poor girl is leading a sort of soundless, inert life in Stein's house. Stein has aged greatly of late. He feels it himself, and says often that he is "preparing to leave all this; preparing to leave . . ." while he waves his hand sadly at his butterflies.
> (416-17)

Works Cited

Batchelor, John. *The Life of Joseph Conrad*. Oxford: Blackwell, 1994.
―――. *Lord Jim*. London: Unwin and Hyman, 1988.
Berthoud, Jacques. *Joseph Conrad: The Major Phase*. Cambridge: Cambridge University Press, 1978.
―――. "Narrative and Ideology: A Critique of Fredric Jameson's *The Political Unconscious*." In *Narrative: From Malory to Motion Pictures*, edited by Jeremy Hawthorn, 101-15. London: Edward Arnold, 1985.
Darwin, Charles. *The Expression of the Emotions in Man and Animals*. London: John Murray, 1890.
Goffman, Erving. "Embarrassment and Social Organization." In *Interaction Ritual*. Harmondsworth: Penguin, 1967.
Ford, Ford Madox. *Joseph Conrad: A Personal Remembrance*. London: Duckworth, 1924.

Harpham, Geoffrey Galt. *One of Us: The Mastery of Joseph Conrad*. Chicago: University of Chicago Press, 1996.
James, Henry. *Embarrassments*. London: Macmillan, 1896.
Jameson, Fredric. *The Political Unconscious: Narrative as a Socially Symbolic Act*. London: Methuen, 1981.
Lange, Robert. "The Eyes Have It: Homoeroticism in *Lord Jim*." *West Virginia University Philological Papers* 38 (1992): 59-68.
Leavis, F. R. *The Great Tradition*. London: Chatto and Windus, 1948.
Morris, Herbert. *On Guilt and Innocence*. Berkeley: University of California Press, 1976.
O'Farrell, Mary Ann. *Telling Complextons: The Nineteenth-Century English Novel and the Blush*. Durham: Duke University Press, 1997.
Peristiany, J. G., ed. *Honour and Shame: The Values of Mediterranean Society*. London: Weidenfeld and Nicolson, 1965.
Piers, Gerhart, and Milton B. Singer. *Shame and Guilt: A Psychoanalytic and Critical Study*. New York: Norton, 1971.
Ricks, Christopher. *Keats and Embarrassment*. Oxford: Clarendon Press, 1974.
Ruppel, Richard. "Joseph Conrad and the Ghost of Oscar Wilde." *The Conradian* 23:1 (1998): 19-36.
Sedgwick, Eve Kosofsky. *Between Men: English Literature and Male Homosocial Desire*. New York: Colombia University Press, 1985.
Stape, J. H., ed. *The Cambridge Critical Companion to Joseph Conrad*. Cambridge: Cambridge University Press, 1996.
Stape, J. H., and Owen Knowles, eds. *A Portrait in Letters: Correspondence to and about Conrad*. Amsterdam – Atlanta, GA.: Rodopi, 1996.
Tanner, Tony. "Butterflies and Beetles – Conrad's Two Truths." In *Lord Jim*, edited by Thomas C. Moser, 447-62. New York: Norton, 1968.
———. "Introduction" to *Pride and Prejudice*. Harmondsworth: Penguin, 1972.
Watt, Ian. *Conrad in the Nineteenth Century*. London: Chatto and Windus, 1980.
———. "Conrad, James and *Chance*." In *Imagined Worlds: Essays on Some English Novels and Novelists in Honour of John Butt*, edited by Maynard Mack and Ian Gregor, 301-22. London: Methuen, 1968.
Watts, Cedric. *Conrad's "Heart of Darkness": A Critical and Contextual Discussion*. Milan: Mursia International, 1977.
———. "The Embarrassing Conrad." Paper presented at 25th International Joseph Conrad Conference of the Joseph Conrad Society (U.K.), University of Kent, Canterbury, July 1999.

BAKHTIN'S MONOLOGISM AND THE ENDINGS OF *CRIME AND PUNISHMENT* AND *LORD JIM*

Cedric Watts
University of Sussex

To become influential, a modern literary theorist apparently needs to deploy erudition, a cluster of impressive key-terms, and some sweeping generalizations. Understandably, then, various critics have used the ideas of Mikhail Bakhtin in their discussions of works by Conrad.[1] Sometimes the notions of "polyphony" and "dialogism" offered in Bakhtin's *Problems of Dostoevsky's Poetics* have been employed. In this essay, I reconsider Bakhtin's claims in the light of a comparison of the endings of *Crime and Punishment* and *Lord Jim*. Given Conrad's explicit hostility to Dostoevsky, there are elements of aptitude and courtesy in such a reconsideration. In any case, the final paragraphs of *Lord Jim* continue to solicit and reward close consideration.

Bakhtin, as the reader will, perhaps a little wearily, recall, contrasted "dialogic" or "polyphonic" texts to "monologic" texts. Although the dialogic does not *supersede* the monologic, the dialogic is nevertheless, Bakhtin claims, the supreme form for the representation of human consciousness: "But again we repeat: *the thinking human consciousness and the dialogic sphere in which this consciousness exists*, in all its depth and specificity, cannot be reached through a monologic artistic approach" (1984, 271).[2] The characteristics of the dialogic text are these: numerous viewpoints are given equal validity, and diverse consciousness are represented, there is "*a plurality of independent and unmerged voices and consciousnesses*"; we encounter the "fundamental open-endedness of the

---

[1] See Aaron Fogel, *Coercion to Speak* (Cambridge, Mass., and London: Harvard University Press, 1985); Gene M. Moore, "Chronotopes and Voices in *Under Western Eyes*," *Conradiana* 18:1 (1986): 9-25; Bruce Henricksen, "The Construction of the Narrator in *The Nigger of the 'Narcissus'*," *PMLA* 103:5 (1988): 783-95; and Daphna Erdinast-Vulcan, *Joseph Conrad and the Modern Temper* (Oxford: Oxford University Press, 1991).

[2] Here and elsewhere, italics within quotations are in the original.

polyphonic novel"; the essence of this artistic world is "rigorous unfinalizability" (6, 39, 272). Which writer exemplified the dialogic? According to Bakhtin, Dostoevsky and only Dostoevsky. Nobody before Dostoevsky managed this, and, furthermore, Bakhtin specifies no "dialogic" authors after Dostoevsky.[3] Even though the first version of Bakhtin's book was published in 1929 and the expanded version was published in 1963, we find not a single reference to Conrad.

Bakhtin tends to conflate the meanings of "dialogic" and "polyphonic," even though to most readers the latter term, which can mean "many-voiced," probably invokes a wider phonic range than the former, which is more likely to invoke the idea of a dialogue between two people (though it is not limited to that connotation). Of course, Bakhtin's general claim about Dostoevsky is reasonably clear and comprehensible. We readily recall the abundant loquacity with which so many Dostoevskian characters present their viewpoints. Russia, in these novels, seems to be populated by individuals impelled by the need to tell their life-stories and confess their sins with remarkable frankness to anyone who will pause to listen. But this very characteristic, this abundant loquacity, helps to give a distinctive Dostoevskian character to Dostoevsky's fiction. If "dialogism" suggests that equal validity is given to each viewpoint – and Bakhtin's phrase "a plurality of fully valid voices" does indeed suggest this – then Dostoevsky is not dialogic. His political and religious biases are evident. He is not neutral but a clear advocate of certain positions. Dostoevsky was a supporter of Tsarism, a hater of Poles, an ardent advocate of Christianity (itself not "dialogic"), and an anti-Semite. In *Crime and Punishment*, the Jewish gate-keeper is described thus by the narrator: "His face wore that perpetual look of peevish dejection which is so sourly printed on all faces of Jewish race without exception" (419). There is no "dialogic" challenge to this depressingly prejudicial generalization. In the same novel, Raskolnikov's redemption comes when, thanks to the love of a good woman, he is persuaded to go down on his knees in public, to confess his crime, repent his sins, and submit to legal punishment; he thus makes a cleansing expiation and prepares himself inwardly for possible recon-

---

[3] Among material dated 1961, entitled "Towards a Reworking of the Dostoevsky Book," Bakhtin rather cryptically notes: "Thomas Mann's *Doktor Faustus* as an indirect confirmation of my idea. Dostoevsky's influence." The notes do not make clear whether Mann should be regarded as achieving the full Dostoevskian polyphony (Bakhtin, 284).

ciliation with God. Certainly he procrastinates and has misgivings before his confession, but the novel becomes "univocal" in endorsing his decision to confess. No persuasive cynic appears at the end to argue that Raskolnikov was misguided and should really have kept quiet. So, in this novel, all ideological positions are obviously not equally valid. A specific position that is conservative in religious (and implicitly in political terms) is clearly advocated.

What does Bakhtin do about this? There is one paragraph in which he recognizes this challenge to his main argument. There he admits that various novels by Dostoevsky, notably *Crime and Punishment*, have a "*conventionally monologic*" ending. So how can this fact be reconciled with his emphasis on the "unfinalizable" nature of the Dovstoevskian project? By saying "We cannot go deeply into this difficult problem here" (39). Neither does he go deeply into it anywhere else. What makes it a "difficult problem" is largely that he has made impossibly extreme claims for Dostoevsky. One implication of his emphasized word "*conventionally*" in that phrase "*conventionally monologic*" is that, here, Dostoevsky is conforming to convention in a way that can be discounted. But if Bakhtin's idea is that the conclusion of *Crime and Punishment* is "tacked on" and may be discounted, it is an idea refuted by the presentation throughout the novel of Raskolnikov as a tormentedly egoistic individual in need of redemption and of Sonia as an altruist whose capacity for redeeming another person can accommodate even the moody murderer.

Bakhtin also concedes that "a novel without an authorial position" is "in general impossible" (67). But Dostoevsky's authorial position (Bakhtin explains) is uniquely generous: he repeatedly gives full autonomy to character after character, like God creating distinctive individuals endowed with free will. The sceptical reader, thinking of the elements of design in the depiction of Raskolnikov's "pilgrim's progress," may prefer to regard Dostoevsky's dialogism not as absolute but relative. It could be said of numerous writers that they permit the expression of a remarkable diversity of views while maintaining "an authorial position." Every literary work has an identity conferred by its author's biases in matters of religion, morality, politics, sexuality, and aesthetics; and every author of more than one text is likely to gain an increasingly evident, if often complex, literary identity generated by family resemblances between his or her different texts. On the other hand, some authors are more capable than others of giving persuasive presentation to viewpoints that may differ from the author's own, or that at least differ from those the author predominantly holds. Similarly, some authors' ideological preferences are sufficiently mixed or variable to result in critical contention about the presence and merits of the those preferences. But to concede this is to concede the oddity of Bakhtin's advocacy, in *Problems of Dostoevsky's Poetics*, of just one writer as representative of the kind of writing that Bakhtin particularly values.

If Dostoevsky's work is polyphonic, then it is evident that other writers are capable of work, or of a body of work, that may be no less polyphonic and possibly even more so. One could cite Chaucer's *Canterbury Tales*, with its diversity of narratives and narrators. Furthermore, being incomplete, the *Canterbury Tales* remains unconcluded, perpetually without resolution and indeed "unfinalizable." Again, Shakespeare is celebrated for the range, richness, complexity, and ambiguity of his works. Shakespeare's own position on a number of important issues – religion, the role of women, political orthodoxy – remains a matter of vigorous debate. If *The Taming of the Shrew* seems patriarchal, *Love's Labour's Lost* seems strikingly feminist. To some commentators, *Richard II* is a politically conservative work (in which the successful usurper, Bolingbroke, experiences guilt and unhappily begins a troubled reign). Others note that the followers of the Earl of Essex arranged for a special production of *Richard II* on the eve of Essex's rebellion, and some contemporaneous spectators (and Queen Elizabeth) clearly believed that the play was subversive. In principle, arguably, a body of plays must be more polyphonic than any novel or body of novels, because a play is a product not only of the author but also (among others) of the actors and their stage-managers or directors, and of the audiences in their variable responses. (The audiences' audible laughter is an important part of a comedy.) Furthermore, being open to excisions, expansions, and other revisions for specific occasions and cultural circumstances, a play is potentially more protean than a novel. Bakhtin concedes that one of his own forerunners in the theory of dialogism was the left-wing critic and novelist Chernyshevsky, who said that Shakespeare "*portrays people and life without saying what he himself thinks on the questions that are resolved by his characters in a way appropriate for each*" (66). In spite of this, Bakhtin denies that polyphony can be found in Shakespeare's dramas: "*authentic polyphony ... did not and could not have existed in ... Shakespeare.*" Bakhtin justifies the denial by declaring that each play "contains only one fully valid voice, the voice of the hero" (178,34). This is obviously untrue of, for instance, *Titus*

Andronicus, Julius Caesar, Troilus and Cressida, Antony and Cleopatra, Coriolanus, the *Henry VI* trilogy, *Richard II, Richard III, 1* and *2 Henry IV, Love's Labour's Lost, As You Like It, Much Ado about Nothing, The Merchant of Venice, Twelfth Night, Measure for Measure, Cymbeline* and *The Winter's Tale.* Indeed, in some of these works it is unclear who, if anyone, is meant to be "the hero."

In another remarkable generalization, Bakhtin alleges that "drama is by its very nature alien to genuine polyphony" (34). This invites the response that whereas a novel usually has a coordinating narrator, a play usually does not. Consequently, "genuine polyphony" may have a greater potential to exist in a play than in a novel. The stage history of, say, *Hamlet* or *Measure for Measure* or *King Lear* suggests this. Arguably, the very amplitude of self-presentation by Dostoevsky's characters reduces the range of interpretive possibilities, whereas Shakespeare leaves gaps that productions can diversely fill. (A good example of such a gap is Isabella's silence, in *Measure for Measure,* when the Duke proposes marriage to her.) If one had to make a list of authors who preceded Dostoevsky and who in their works seem at least as polyphonic, and possibly more so than he, one would think not only of Chaucer and Shakespeare but also of, for example, Aeschylus, Euripides, Webster, Defoe, Swift, Richardson, and Emily Brontë. Famously, one of George Eliot's projects in *Middlemarch* was to demonstrate that each individual needs to recognize the "equivalent centre of self" (225) in another individual. Bakhtin deals with this kind of argument by means of a wobbly assertion of Dostoevsky's singularity:

> Dostoevsky is the creator of *authentic polyphony,* which, of course, did not and could not have existed in the Socratic dialogue, the ancient Menippean satire, the medieval mystery play, in Shakespeare and Cervantes, Voltaire and Diderot, Balzac and Hugo. But polyphony was prepared for in a *fundamental* way by this line of development. ... This entire tradition ... was reborn and renewed in Dostoevsky in the uniquely original and innovative form of the polyphonic novel.   (178)

The "wobble" appears in the apparent concession that "in a *fundamental* way" those early writers anticipated polyphony. But instead of inspecting the implications of this, instead of recognizing that Dostoevsky was not unique but merely one of many presenters of the dialogic, Bakhtin falls back on his customary claim that Dostoevsky was "uniquely original."

The fatal flaw of Bakhtin's discussion is that it is relentlessly *monologic*. It fails to give appropriate attention to feasible counter-arguments and, again and again, asserts Dostoevsky's dialogic or polyphonic singularity. At the same time, the suggestion that polyphony is valuable is repeatedly subverted by Bakhtin, who, resisting various opportunities for polyphony in his own argument, shows that he is really a devotee of the monologic monograph.

Bakhtin's monologism is clearly exposed by a consideration of *Lord Jim*. As is widely recognized, one of the most "modernistic" features of *Lord Jim* is found in the first half of the novel, when diverse characters offers a diversity of comments, explicit and implicit, on Jim, and thereby reveal their own moral or ideological principles or prejudices. Jim is depicted as an enigma, as someone difficult to sum up. Repeatedly we are told that he is "under a cloud": a characteristically ambiguous phrase, meaning both that he is overshadowed by disgrace and that he is hard to make out. Famously, Stein's attempt to sum him up results in statements that shimmer on the borderline between paradox and contradiction. Jim is romantic, which is "very bad.... Very good, too" (216). "But *is he*?" asks Marlow, compounding the "dialogism" of the scene. Stein's central statement is famously delphic:

> "Very funny this terrible thing is. A man that is born falls into a dream like a man who falls into the sea. If he tries to climb out into the air as inexperienced people endeavour to do, he drowns – *nicht wahr?* . . . No! I tell you! The way is to the destructive element submit yourself, and with the exertions of your hands and feet in the water make the deep, deep sea keep you up." (214)

The speech permits quite contradictory glosses.[4] One is this: "It's both comical and tragic. Every man who is born into the dream that we call real life is like a man who falls into the sea. If he conceives exalted aspirations and tries to escape from mundane reality, he's like an inexperienced swimmer who, panicking, tries to climb up into the air and consequently drowns. The experienced swimmer, on the other hand, survives by co-operating with the sea: he treads water and lets it sustain him. Similarly, the practical man survives by adapting to reality and co-operating with it." The contradictory gloss is this: "It's both comical and tragic. Every man

---

[4] Here I quote my notes in *Lord Jim*, Watts and Hampson, eds., 360.

who is born enters the realm of ambitions and ideals as inevitably as someone falling into the sea. If he tries to evade those dreams, he perishes. He must come to terms with them, work with them, and thus survive." So the speech can be reduced to a contradiction: "Be a realist, not an idealist; yet be an idealist, not a realist." It thus sums up, without really resolving, the central themes, tensions, and problems of the novel. Understandable, then, though resistible, is the temptation to suggest that dialogism is a topic of the novel and polyphony is its mode.

There may possibly be some debts to *Crime and Punishment*. We are told of Raskolnikov in prison:

> He could have borne anything then, even shame and disgrace. But he judged himself severely, and his exasperated conscience found no particularly terrible fault in his past, except a simple *blunder* which might happen to anyone. He was ashamed just because he, Raskolnikov, had so hopelessly, stupidly come to grief through some decree of blind fate, and must humble himself and submit to "the idiocy" of a sentence, if he were anyhow to be at peace. (442)

This is not unlike Jim's attitude to the Court of Inquiry. Jim, too, is inclined to regard his culpable act as a blunder that might happen to anyone ("You think me a cur ... but what would you have done?" [92]); he, too, feels that fate has victimized him ("what a chance missed!"; "infernal powers ... had selected him for the victim of their practical joke" [83,108]) and that the court's proceedings are idiotic ("All these staring people in court seemed such fools"; "They demanded facts from him, as if facts could explain anything" [76,29]). One important difference, however, is the presence of Marlow as partly sympathetic and partly critical interrogator of Jim, constantly generalizing the problems and probing Jim's attitudes. Characteristically, when Jim says "There was not the thickness of a sheet of paper between the right and the wrong of this affair," Marlow responds: "How much more did you want?" (130).

Bakhtin stresses the importance of open-endedness while paradoxically discounting the evidence of "completedness," as he puts it, in Dostoevsky's fiction; so some comparison of the endings of *Crime and Punishment* and *Lord Jim* is appropriate here. In the closing pages of *Crime and Punishment*, we know that Raskolnikov and the loving Sonia believe that at the end of his remarkably lenient eight-year sentence for the double murder they will be united. He is at last able to reciprocate Sonia's feelings:

> [Their] sick pale faces were bright with the dawn of a new future, of a full resurrection into a new life. They were renewed by love: the heart of each held infinite sources of life for the heart of the other. ... [H]e had risen again ... Life had stepped into the place of theory ...   (447-48)

Later, he sits holding her copy of the New Testament:

> He did not open it now, but one thought passed through his mind: "Can her convictions not be mine now? Her feelings, her aspirations at least..."
> She too had been greatly agitated that day, and at night she was taken ill again. But she was so happy – and so unexpectedly happy – that she was almost frightened of her happiness. Seven years, *only* seven years! At the beginning of their happiness at some moments they were both ready to look on those seven years as though they were seven days. He did not know that the new life would not be given him for nothing, that he would have to pay dearly for it, that it would cost him great striving, great suffering.
> But that is the beginning of a new story – the story of the gradual renewal of a man, the story of his gradual regeneration, of his passing from one world into another, of his initiation into a new unknown life. That might be the subject of a new story, but our present story is ended.
> (448)

One prominent feature of this ending is indeed its conventionality. At long last, love prevails. Sonia wins reciprocal feeling from the man she has long served. The discovery of love is, for Raskolnikov, the source of regeneration. Life triumphs over his arid theory. The biblical imagery (resurrection, a rising again from the dead) emphasizes the joyous significance of the occasion. Raskolnikov is a man reborn. There's no dissenting voice: a turning-point for the better has been reached. Like other nineteenth-century novelists – Dickens in *Hard Times*, for example, or George Eliot in *Middlemarch* – the author looks into the crystal ball and tells the fortunes of the main characters. The anonymous but evidently authoritative narrator of *Crime and Punishment* is a traditional omniscience with knowledge of the future; and what is emphasized is that, though suffering awaits Raskolnikov, his gradual regeneration will proceed. Like Mr. Rochester in *Jane Eyre*, the sinner will be born again, thanks to the forgiveness and love of a good woman. As if to mock Bakhtin, the ending is not a contradiction of what has preceded it in *Crime and Punishment*; on the contrary, the developing relationship between Raskolnikov and Sonia, the general theme of the quest for atonement and salvation in various lives, and the very title of the novel itself, have prepared us for some such conclusion.

Here, in turn, are the paragraphs of *Lord Jim* that, after the account of Jim's death, conclude the novel:

> "And that's the end. He passes away under a cloud, inscrutable at heart, forgotten, unforgiven, and excessively romantic. Not in the wildest days of his boyish visions could he have seen the alluring shape of such an extraordinary success! For it may very well be that in the short moment of his last proud and unflinching glance, he had beheld the face of that opportunity which, like an Eastern bride, had come veiled to his side.
>
> But we can see him, an obscure conqueror of fame, tearing himself out of the arms of a jealous love at the sign, at the call of his exalted egoism. He goes away from a living woman to celebrate his pitiless wedding with a shadowy ideal of conduct. Is he satisfied – quite, now, I wonder? We ought to know. He is one of us – and have I not stood up once, like an evoked ghost, to answer for his eternal constancy? Was I so very wrong after all? Now he is no more, there are days when the reality of his existence comes to me with an immense, with an overwhelming force; and yet upon my honour there are moments, too, when he passes from my eyes like a disembodied spirit astray amongst the passions of this earth, ready to surrender himself faithfully to the claim of his own world of shades.
>
> Who knows? He is gone, inscrutable at heart, and the poor girl is leading a sort of soundless, inert life at Stein's house. Stein has aged greatly of late. He feels it himself, and says often that he is 'preparing to leave all this; preparing to leave . . .' while he waves his hand sadly at his butterflies."   (416-17)

In one obvious sense, the novel has had its closure: the story of Jim's career is concluded with Jim's death. In an equally obvious sense, it remains open-ended, for the evaluation of Jim continues, and some questions remain unanswered and possibly unanswerable. Question-marks are recurrent here, as they are not in Dostoevsky's paragraphs. Marlow speculates that Jim may at last have beheld the "face" of his opportunity, a face that previously was veiled. Perhaps Jim has at last demonstrated that he can be honourably courageous and has thus realized his self-image and atoned for his act of cowardice. This time he has not run away; he has not deserted those non-Europeans towards whom he feels he bears responsibility. On the other hand, what kind of face has been unveiled? One of Conrad's source-books, McNair's *Perak and the Malays*, remarks that, at a Malay wedding feast, "if the lady, on being unveiled, prove to be very plain, the bridegroom is bantered and laughed at unmercifully" (1878, 233).

Marlow suggests that "we" can see Jim as guilty of infidelity. He has turned away from "a jealous love" (Jewel's love for him) to that bride who can be interpreted as merely "exalted egoism": the apparently altruistic death, an atonement to others, can be seen as an egoistic death, a vindication of pride and romantic ambition. (In Chapter 24 we were told that Jim "seemed to love the land and the people with a sort of fierce egoism" [248].) His "ideal of conduct" is shadowy, and he has given it priority over "a living woman." The question "Is he satisfied – quite, now, I wonder?" subverts the sense that Jim's biography concludes with his death. The question about Jim's possible feelings "now" extends the action into a hypothesized afterlife. The declaration "He is one of us" repeats a familiar leitmotif of the novel and a characteristically ambiguous one, since the phrase has variously meant "a fellow-gentleman," "a white gentleman," "a white man," "an outwardly-honest Englishman," "a good seaman," "an ordinary person," and "a fellow human being."

Marlow then asks the double question: "have I not stood up ... to answer for his eternal constancy? Was I so very wrong after all?" The answer to the first question is "Yes": that was in Chapter 33, when he had assured Jewel that nothing and nobody could take Jim from her side. The answer to the second question is "Yes and no," for Jim has indeed left her; but she, it seems certain, will never forget him: he will haunt her reflections. The status of the word "eternal" hovers ambiguously between hyperbole (as in such idioms as "You have my eternal gratitude") and an allusion to an assumed real afterlife. Sometimes, says Marlow, Jim's existence seems immensely real – but Marlow immediately supplies the other half of the paradox: sometimes, too, he seems a disembodied spirit, not substantial but ghostly. Yet he is "a disembodied spirit astray among the passions of this earth" – a ghost among the passions of this world. What that means is particularly elusive. One could give it a secular gloss. Whereas at times he seems solidly real, at other times, as memory fades, he drifts vaguely among emotionally tinged recollections, or among human sufferings, if one adopts the root meaning of "passions." Does that mean that what Jim represented may be considered as living on, or being considered in relationship to, the continuing emotions of humankind? But the disembodied spirit is "ready to surrender himself faithfully to the claim of his own world of shades." This may be a poetical way of saying that he enters oblivion, that he becomes forgotten.[5] The classical imagery of "shades," the spirits of the dead in an afterlife, is recurrent in Conrad's works, and here may permit us to imagine also that Jim's spirit is as consistent in death as it was in life. One gloss is that, in life, he may have thought that finally he committed himself faithfully to the claims, the moral justice, of Doramin and his fellows; in death, he may regard himself as surrendering faithfully to whatever his fellow-ghosts may demand of him. In this sequence the often sceptical Marlow, like a tolerant agnostic, entertains the thought of a supernatural afterlife and speculates on its nature. A complication is caused by the way in which the phrasing precisely echoes that at the end of a sentence in Chapter 33: "Thus a poor mortal seduced by the charm of an apparition might have tried to wring from another ghost the tremendous secret of the claim the other world holds over a disembodied soul astray amongst the passions of this earth" (315). The imagery is supernatural, but the topic is whether Marlow, from the West, can tell Jewel the secret of Jim's past. The *Patna* scandal, and not some occult power exerted by Hadean ghosts, may be the "tremendous secret." Therefore, in the novel's penultimate paragraph, Marlow's imagery is both speculatively predictive and ironically retrospective.

At the beginning of the final paragraph, Marlow's agnosticism is emphasized in the question, "Who knows?" Who can pronounce any closure? So Jim remains "inscrutable at heart": the long quest to resolve the enigma of his character remains unconcluded. As for Jewel: "the poor girl is leading a sort of soundless, inert life in Stein's house." If Jim was loyal to one ideal, he can be seen as disloyal to another – honouring Jewel's claims on his devotion. Jim and Marlow had promised Jewel that Jim would not leave her; but, in her eyes, he has indeed left her – for ever. She and Tamb' Itam had urged him to stand and fight, in the hope of escaping. "Jumping ship," in both literal and metaphorical terms, has

---

5 Marlow has referred to Jim as "my brother from the realm of forgetful shades" (316), that realm being perhaps the west, or, more specifically, people who had known Jim in the past but were in process of forgetting him.

become a theme of this novel. Once Jim had stood still when he should have jumped (from a training ship into its boat, to effect a rescue); later, he had jumped (from the *Patna*) when he should have stood still; on Patusan he had rightly escaped from captivity by a leap; finally, he stays when Jewel thinks he should have escaped ("jumped ship") from Patusan. Now, Jewel, the orphan, is further isolated and is disillusioned, exiled, mute, and drained of energy. Stein, in turn, has "aged greatly of late," for his experiment with Marlow to arrange Jim's regeneration has had disastrous consequences. He prepares for his own death, a departure from his collection of butterflies – creatures once rare, beautiful and living, but now dead and pinned in the collector's trays. To catch their fluttering beauty is to destroy it; they no longer flutter, and the colours fade. To seize and preserve is to kill. In pinning the butterfly down, to capture it is to lose it. This can be treated as a comment on Jim and on the novel itself. Marlow recognizes that to resolve Jim's nature would entail being able to give the final word; but to give the final word would entail closing down the life, pinning down – or nailing down – the character. As D. H. Lawrence says, "If you try to nail anything down in the novel, either it kills the novel, or the novel gets up and walks away with the nail" (1970, 528). A typical (because paradoxical) complication in *Lord Jim* is that Stein has envisaged the butterfly as content with stasis, for it "sits still" on its "heap of dirt" (213), in contrast to men, who rashly strive incessantly for the unrealisable.

The last punctuation-mark in *Lord Jim* is a closing quotation-mark. But this closing opens. The quotation-mark reminds us that these "last words" of the novel are not an omniscient narrator's, but are Captain Charles Marlow's. He, you will recall, had finished his oral narrative at the end of Chapter 35. In the following chapters, the story of Jim is continued by means of three letters (one by Jim, one by his father, and one by Marlow) and a lengthy report by Marlow that is ostensibly based on information provided by Brown, Stein, Jewel, and Tamb' Itam. All this written material is supposedly being read by a "privileged man" in the heart of a great city, presumably London; a man who had criticized Jim's career on Patusan by arguing on imperialistic lines. Marlow writes to and of him:

> You said also – I call to mind – that "giving your life up to them" (*them* meaning all of mankind with skins brown, yellow, or black in colour) "was like selling your soul to a brute." You contended that "that kind of thing" was only endurable and enduring when based on a firm convic-

tion in the truth of ideas racially our own, in whose name are established the order, the morality of an ethical progress. "We want its strength at our backs," you had said. "We want a belief in its necessity and its justice, to make a worthy and conscious sacrifice of our lives. Without it the sacrifice is only forgetfulness, the way of offering is no better than the way to perdition.' ... The point, however, is that of all mankind Jim had no dealings but with himself, and the question is whether at the last he had not confessed to a faith mightier than the laws of order and progress.

I affirm nothing. (339)

Thus, as introduced by Marlow, the documents that tell the story of the end of Jim's life are presented as evidence within a large debate about the nature and value of Jim's career when measured against certain specific political and moral criteria; and those criteria, in turn, are being appraised. That Marlow says "I affirm nothing" is consistent with the ambiguities of the novel's close. Marlow is, at times, evidently unreliable. The statement that "Jim had no dealings but with himself" is untrue. It is a hyperbolic way of saying that egoism is a large element in Jim's character; but two marked features of Jim's period in Patusan are, first, his considerate, well-intentioned interaction with Dain Waris and his people, and, secondly, his love-relationship with Jewel. Jim's romantic dreams need a responding community for their fulfilment. If egoistic ambition entails helping and gratifying others, it becomes sufficiently altruistic.

On the other side, if we consider the arguments of the privileged man, we find that their gist is that individualistic benevolent paternalism abroad most often results in disaster. Involvement with imperialism, which is a concerted effort, may contribute to "ethical progress," but the lone quester may experience "weariness and ... disgust with acquired honour, with the self-appointed task, with the love sprung from pity and youth," and may even find that he has sold his soul "to a brute" (338, 339). Now this privileged man makes evident his racial prejudice and his faith in large-scale imperialism; but his arguments cannot be entirely dismissed. If there had been no encounter with Brown, and Jim had lived, his youthful enthusiasm might well have faded, and he might have experienced various kinds of disgust or disillusionment. The text hints at ways in which they might develop. He might become disgusted by having to deal with numerous local disputes that are often petty and bewildering: "The trouble was to get at the truth of anything" (269). There might be friction with Doramin, who has treasured hopes of his son's emergence as ruler, and whose attitude to Jim has been watchful, wary, distrustful, and even jealous. Other Conradian narratives have shown how the enthusiasm of a benevolent patron abroad may lead to degrees of disillusionment. Lingard and Gould exhibit it; and of course Kurtz had gone to Africa with ideals, with a sense of a benevolent mission. If Jim had been part of a large-scale British endeavour to colonize Patusan, Brown could not have posed the threat that he did. The privileged man's basic prediction that Jim's endeavour is doomed is indeed fulfilled, even if the actual event does not correspond to the detail of his prediction.

Marlow asks whether, finally, Jim "had not confessed to a faith mightier than the laws of order and progress." In what could this "mightier faith" consist? Marlow doesn't spell it out, and guesses will vary from reader to reader. "A sense of brotherhood" might be one answer; "self-sacrificing love" might be another; "a sense of honour so great that death is to be preferred to dishonour" might be another. But are not such matters part of "the laws of order and progress"? If not, shouldn't they be? What are those laws, exactly? In such ways, the material in the closing chapter functions as part of a debate about empire, morality, and identity; and the modes of presentation magnify the complexity and ambiguity.

The "privileged listener" was, we are told, one of the group of Marlow's auditors, one of those who had heard the tale of Jim (the narrative of Chapters 5 to 35 inclusive). He is the "only ... man of all these listeners who was ever to hear the last word of the story" (337). But who is telling us this? An anonymous narrator has been present from the start and is now telling us of the unique status of the privileged man. But if the privileged man is the only person who ever hears the end of the story, it follows that the anonymous narrator is not a character but a disembodied commenting self, rather like a traditional omniscient narrator – except that this person is peculiarly self-effacing. He grants the concluding chapters, after the first four paragraphs of Chapter 36, entirely to Marlow, and, as we have seen, makes no comment when Marlow's narrative is complete. Where a more conventional novelist would have let the disembodied narrator sum matters up, Conrad here denies him that role. Consequently, the ending of *Lord Jim* is far more open-ended, and conspicuously thus, than is the ending of *Crime and Punishment*; and what's more, *Lord Jim* has a concluding narrative strategy that encourages us to weigh up the later evidence against the earlier claims and forewarnings by the privileged man, against the hopes of Stein and the earlier reflections by Marlow. As Marlow had observed, "the last word is not said – probably shall never be said. Are not our lives too short for that full utterance ...?" (225) And in any case, of what value is the last word? Marlow's scepticism has anticipated even that, remarking: "words also belong to the sheltering conception of light and order which is our refuge": outside it lies "the chaos of dark thoughts ... beyond the pale" (313).

In *Crime and Punishment*, an unambiguous moral reference-point is provided by the shining redemptive virtue of Sonia, a Mary Magdalen figure, the "fallen woman" who emerges as the soul-saving angel for Raskolnikov. No such unambiguous reference-point is provided in *Lord Jim*. Jewel loves Jim and intervenes on at least one occasion to save his life; but her endeavour to save him after the encounter with Gentleman Brown is unavailing, and she is finally saddened if not embittered by Jim's choice of death at the hand of Doramin rather than staying by her side. Marlow has befriended and helped Jim, but it is Marlow who maintains a critical discussion of the significance of Jim's character and career, a discussion that, as we have seen, he conspicuously does not conclude with a decisive judgement. Of course *Lord Jim* is not fully dialogic or fully polyphonic (what text is?), for certain Conradian preoccupations and thematic concerns clearly direct the novel. Like the vast majority of novelists, Conrad commends virtue and condemns vice: kindness, charity, and honour are upheld, while cruelty, meanness, and treachery are condemned. Nevertheless, one can reasonably argue that *Lord Jim* is more dialogic and polyphonic than is *Crime and Punishment*.

Lord Jim, therefore, enables us to criticize Bakhtin's theoretical propositions in the following ways. First, his definition of the dialogic and polyphonic novel is at once too vague and too schematic. Secondly, Bakhtin is peculiarly myopic in seeing only Dostoevsky as the creator of "an artistic world" that has "rigorous unfinalizability and dialogic openness" (272). Numerous authors have generated works that, individually or combined as an *œuvre*, have as much or more of these qualities. Bakhtin's failure to consider Conrad or even to mention him is a sign of a larger inadequacy. Two technical adjectives – "dialogic" and "polyphonic" – were, for better or for worse, certainly helped into fashionability by the translation of Bakhtin's book, and have been found variously useful. But the book's main topic, the advocacy of works that are richly ambiguous, complex, and multivocal, was not original. Such an interest can be found in the writings of numerous critics who gained fame before Bakhtin (among them Hazlitt, Pater, and Wilde), in Keats's letters, and in the output of such poets as Blake, Tennyson, and Browning. In Russia, Shklovsky had already emphasized the "multi-voiced" quality of Dostoevsky's fiction (Bakhtin 39). Bakhtin's *Problems of Dostoevsky's Poetics* became widely known and much discussed in the 1980s; but before that decade, many aspects of what he termed the dialogic and the polyphonic had been considered by writers as varied as Lawrence, Eliot, Empson, Cleanth Brooks, Wimsatt, and Beardsley. More recently, Barthes, Foucault, Derrida, and their followers have propagated the notion that any text is inherently polyphonic, being a play of signs intoxicated by *différance*, and may, indeed, mean whatever any reader takes it to mean (unless it be a text of his or her own, which of course transcends this confusion); so we must hope that such deconstructionism is not adopted by chefs, pharmacists, policemen, accountants, and undertakers. What is of value in Bakhtin's book was already available in the works of others: notably, in the literary practice of Joseph Conrad in *Lord Jim*. In any case, one of the most lucid statements of the need for and value of the polyphonic is to be found not in Bakhtin's somewhat prolix pages but in Conrad's concise letter to the *New York Times* in 1901. That is the letter in which he declares: "the business of a work striving to be art is not to teach or to prophesy ... nor yet to pronounce a definite conclusion. ... The only legitimate basis of creative work lies in the courageous recognition of all the irreconcilable antagonisms that make our life so enigmatic, so burdensome, so fascinating, so dangerous – so full of hope. They exist! And this is the only fundamental truth of fiction" (*CL2* 348-49).

Works Cited

Bakhtin, Mikhail. *Problems of Dostoevsky's Poetics*. Edited and Translated by Caryl Emerson. Manchester: Manchester University Press, 1984.
Conrad, Joseph. *Lord Jim*. Edited by Cedric Watts and Robert Hampson. London: Penguin, 1986. Reprint, 1989.
Dostoevsky, Fyodor. *Crime and Punishment*. Translated by Constance Garnett. London: Heinemann, 1914. Reprint, London: Landsborough, 1958.
Eliot, George. *Middlemarch*. London: Oxford University Press, 1947.
Lawrence, D. H. "Morality and the Novel." In *Phoenix* [Vol. 1]. London: Heinemann, 1936. Reprint, 1970.
McNair, Major Fred. *Perak and the Malays*. London: Tinsley Brothers, 1878.

"He was misleading": Frustrated Gestures in *Lord Jim*

Allan H. Simmons
St. Mary's College, Strawberry Hill

> The views he let me have of himself were like those glimpses through the shifting rents in a thick fog – bits of vivid and vanishing detail, giving no connected idea of the general aspect of a country. They fed one's curiosity without satisfying it; they were no good for purposes of orientation. Upon the whole he was misleading. (76)

Lord Jim advertises its concern with the troubled identity of its central character from its very title, that combines the honorific "Lord" with the demotic "Jim," suggesting that Jim's identity lies somewhere between these two signifiers. This concern is then reinforced in the two-part structure of the novel – its *Patna* and Patusan halves – together with the range of opinions offered on the "case" (212) of Jim, suggesting that the questions raised about his character will be eventually answered. In fact, this structural pattern proves to be deceptive and Marlow's narrative concludes with a question: "Is he satisfied – quite, now, I wonder?" (416). This, at the end of a process that begins with the substitution of the detached frame-narrator by Marlow, together with the implicit rejection of objective "facts" about Jim in favour of subjective, sympathetic understanding, leads the reader to expect an answer to the riddle posed by Jim's character, only to confound this expectation. In the novel's early chapters, narrative strategies announce that information is being withheld, creating an implicit demand for Marlow, whose presence, coupled with Jim's second chance on Patusan, lead us to expect an answer to the questions posed by Jim's character. Instead, delay and deferral ensure that final meaning is suspended indefinitely. *Lord Jim* comprises a search for truth but ends with Stein's gnomic experiment (that, like the "facts" Marlow dismisses, can't explain everything either). Ultimately, the novel is based on a paradox that invites us to admire commitment to an ideal that can never be justified: the quest for an underlying moral truth that will somehow explain Jim implies the belief that such a truth exists; yet the belief itself is unsustainable.

So, structurally, *Lord Jim* might be said to be composed of frustrated anticipatory gestures that predict the tale and are then confounded. As Marlow says of Jim, we can say of the narrative generally: upon the whole it is misleading. In this essay I shall first consider the misleading nature of the narrative's anticipatory techniques – its proleptic gestures – and then, starting with the "light holiday literature" (5) upon which Jim's maritime career is predicated, explore the manner in which *Lord Jim* self consciously calls attention to the fictions that generate it.

To start with, I should like to consider the broad structural patterns of this narrative. It begins with an omniscient narrator who first introduces Jim and the mysterious, unspecified "fact" (4) from which he is fleeing, and then proceeds to trace Jim's maritime career from the training-ship through to the *Patna* incident and the subsequent "official Inquiry" (28), where the very "fact" that we have been pursuing is reduced to the status of a red herring: "They wanted facts. Facts! They demanded facts from him, as if facts could explain anything!" (29). Here, the free indirect discourse confers narratorial endorsement upon Jim's exasperation while simultaneously deflecting the reader's original quest for "facts." Marlow's subsequent assurance that there was "no incertitude as to facts" and his reference to the "the well known fact" (56), which is none the less withheld, reinforce this by suggesting that facts are not worth pursuing anyway. But facts in the novel nonetheless continue to exert a certain mesmerizing power, perhaps even offer an anchor against Jim's overactive imagination. (One wonders whether Marlow overly identifies with Jim's point of view here for, as his own narration confirms, while facts may not explain anything they do count – as witness his own response to the guano-island proposal.) If, as Jonathan Culler argues, "the desire to see an enigma or problem resolved [leads] one to organize sequences so as to make them satisfy" (1975, 211), then this narrative deliberately misleads us, for our reading of the opening is structured around a succession of questions, posed with increasing precision, that culminate when we are able to ask: What *fact* is Jim concealing?

Considered as a whole (or macrostructurally), the novel's unity depends upon our being able to see the relevance of the *Patna* and Patusan "halves" – and Patusan's status as either a mental hideaway or an actual place where Jim regenerates himself through action depends upon this.

Writing to Edward Garnett in November 1900, Conrad said: "you've put your finger on the plague spot. The division of the book into two parts" (*CL2* 302). Subsequent criticism remains divided over the unity of these two parts, either endorsing the causal justification for Patusan or arguing that it is neither necessitated by nor able to sustain the intensity of the *Patna* sequence.[1] Of course, the narrative fissures in *Lord Jim* relate to the improvisatory techniques Conrad employed when composing the novel for serialization.[2] My concern here, however, is not with the novel's composition but with the reading process determined by its final form.

No other strategy so defines Conrad's attempt to reconcile the novel's two parts as his use of anticipatory gestures. For instance, the word "Patusan" obviously carries echoes of the word "Patna." More subtly, the reader gets the impression that the various narratives and narrators are in cahoots. So, Marlow's opening words, "Oh yes. I attended the inquiry" (34), appear to be solicited by the omniscient narrator's description of him as the "white man who sat apart from the others ... with quiet eyes that glanced straight, interested and clear" (32), while his comment "Then it was our glances met" (69) links two narratives (echoing the omniscient narration's claim that Jim "met the eyes of the white man" [32]), suggesting metafictional dialogue between them. Into this category of prolepsis fall such examples as Marlow wanting Jim "impaled like a beetle" (42) – an image that anticipates both the Stein interview and the taking of Sherif Ali's fortress, during which Dain Waris saved Jim from being "pinned" with a spear "to a baulk of timber like one of Stein's beetles" (270) – the "muffled detonation" (131) made when Jim strikes his chest, his grimly prophetic exclamation "May I be shot" (107), and the atmospheric connection between Stein's study and Patusan (204). Even the issue of Jim's identity mentioned earlier is affected, as the omniscient narrator's observation "They called him Tuan Jim: as one might say – Lord Jim" (5) is an echo of Cornelius's words to Brown: "Tuan Jim. As you may say Lord Jim" (367). There is a sense in which this text seems to be listening in to itself generating itself.

---

[1] See Tanner (1973) 10, and Leavis (1948) 190.
[2] Consider, for instance, Stape's argument that the ending of the novel was to have been Marlow's last glimpse of Patusan in Chapter 35 and, thus, that the whole of the Patusan sequence, drafted between mid-May and early July 1900, may not have been conceived as a dramatized element much before the writing of it began.

Such thematic and structural anticipatory gestures awaken our interest in proleptic patterns generally and, as Frank Kermode argues, "Once a certain kind of attention has been aroused we read according to the values appropriate to that kind of attention whether or no there is a series of gestures to prompt us" (1983, 57). As every reader of *Lord Jim* discovers, preparatory comments are inscribed everywhere in the narrative. Thus, Marlow first sees Jim looking at the Malabar House "with the air of a man about to go for a walk as soon as his friend is ready" (42), a description soon realized at the quay-side after the Inquiry, when Marlow finds Jim "as though he had been waiting for me there to come along and carry him off" (171). On a broader scale, Brierly's "Let him creep twenty feet underground and stay there" and, more subtly, "Why eat all that dirt?" (66) both prefigure Jim's fate on Patusan, where, in his escape from the Rajah's stockade, he does actually eat dirt (254). In each case, what commences as figural language becomes literal, the figure is realized, and so has to be reinterpreted as having an anticipatory dimension.

The degree to which the narrative is composed of such figures is found in the fine detail. To appreciate just how fine, consider how the moments aboard the *Patna* immediately before the collision connect what we know of the preceding sequences of Jim's maritime career. After the storm at sea during which he is lamed by the falling spar, Jim is described as lying in his cabin "as if at the bottom of an abyss of unrest" (11). Then, on the *Patna* voyage, days pass "as if falling into an abyss for ever open in the wake of the ship" (16). And then this "abyss," which constitutes an experience replicated in the reading process itself, issues naturally into the "everlastingly deep hole" (111) into which Jim says he has jumped. So we are encouraged to read the narrative in terms of such associations. Even more subtly, the pencil used to mark the *Patna*'s exact location is described as looking "like a naked ship's spar floating in the pool of a sheltered dock" (20), a comparison that invokes both the storm at sea and the training-ship incident. This accumulation of ideas occurs just after the reference to the (unspecified) "coming event" (19), inviting us to predict, in the chain of inference, Jim's response to the crisis. Clearly, like Jane Austen, Conrad does "not write for such dull Elves / As have not a great deal of Ingenuity themselves" (letter to Cassandra Austen, dated 29 January 1813).

The degree to which the narrative information we receive is both cumulative and disorientating can be seen in the following short sequence from the training-ship incident where, as he arrives on deck in response to the injunction "Something's up. Come along" (6), Jim holds his breath "in awe" and is "whirled around":

> He was jostled. "Man the cutter!" Boys rushed past him. A coaster running in for shelter had crashed through a schooner at anchor, and one of the ship's instructors had seen the accident. A mob of boys clambered on the rails, clustered round the davits. "Collision. Just ahead of us. Mr. Symons saw it." A push made him stagger against the mizzen-mast, and he caught hold of a rope. The old training-ship chained to her moorings quivered all over, bowing gently head to wind, and with her scant rigging humming in a deep bass the breathless song of her youth at sea. "Lower away!" He saw the boat, manned, drop swiftly below the rail, and rushed after her. (7)

The variable perspective, which carries the suggestion of Jim's own bewilderment, anticipates the range of different narrators in *Lord Jim*, each of whom creates another prism in the mist through which the reader sees Jim. The passage confounds both temporal and causal sequences, leaving it up to the reader to differentiate between consecution and consequence.[3] Here is a brief analysis of the same passage, sentence by sentence (numbered):

(1)	He was jostled.	Since there is no way of knowing whether this explains Jim's impression of being "whirled around," the reader is placed *in medias res*, conscious of limited knowledge whilst anticipating action. The passive verb suggests the passivity of the subject, disturbed from a more comfortable state, whilst the choice of the verb suggests his indignation.
(2)	"Man the cutter!"	However unsure we are about what has occasioned it, the command implies a sequence: we expect it to be obeyed. Direct speech injects dramatic intensity

---

[3] Barthes suggests that this confusion between what comes *after* and what is *caused by* provides "the mainspring of narrative" (1977, 94).

		into the scene but, while this reduces the narrative distance between the reader and the action, it also emphasizes the readers' disorientation: we converge on the narrative through the words of an unidentified speaker.
(3)	Boys rushed past him.	This sentence simultaneously extends the passivity and immobility of Jim, hinted at in (1), and indicates an immediate response to the order in (2) on the part of others. The urgency of the verb propels the reader forward, expecting something to happen.
(4)	A coaster running in for shelter had crashed through a schooner at anchor, and one of the ship's instructors had seen the accident.	At last, the enigma isolated by the injunction "Something's up" is now identified. This analeptic (and omniscient) summary thus provides a context for the order given in (2) but checks the momentum anticipated in (3). By providing a contrast to the pattern of fragmentary and restricted focalizations through which the rescue is being filtered, the increased distance and relative length of this summary reinforce the impression that the prose is informative but not totally so.
(5)	A mob of boys clambered on the rails, clustered round the davits.	A further consequence of the command in (2), this action extends that described in (3). Jim's absence is, again, conspicuous – made more so by the alliterative associative verbs "clambered" and "clustered," which also suggest disorder. The diction – "jostled" in (1) is extended through the choice of the word "mob" here – renders focalization ambiguous: its tone insinuates Jim's sense of inner superiority into the narratorial perspective.

(6)	"Collision. Just ahead of us. Mr. Symons saw it."	The summary in (4) is now restated within the field of action as the clipped phrases of direct speech create the illusion of immediacy through their sense of breathlessness. That these words are not attributable to any identifiable character lends them a choric quality: they become the voice or atmosphere of "the boys."
(7)	A push made him stagger against the mizzen-mast, and he caught hold of a rope.	The bifurcation of narrative continues. Although Jim is our focus, we are aware that action is taking place around him. This inverts the perspectival balance of (5) where Jim's inaction was implied by the action of his fellows. Whilst Jim's act – catching hold of the rope – is involuntary, a reflex to prevent him from falling, the sense of action taking place around him continues. The use of "push" amplifies and repeats "jostled" in (1), both words combining to suggest Jim's dream-like state of unawareness that is impacted on by reality and action.
(8)	The old training-ship chained to her moorings quivered all over, bowing gently head to wind, and with her scant rigging humming in a deep bass the breathless song of her youth at sea.	Once again, the unfolding rescue drama is checked. Like the summary in (4), it is presented from a detached perspective, but unlike (4) its tone is not immediately discoverable. Its romanticism seems rooted in the poetic imagination we are already beginning to associate with Jim; its calm detachment, on the other hand, is inconsistent with his sense of "awe."
(9)	"Lower away!"	As with (2), we expect this command to initiate a sequence of actions. Its urgency hurries the reader forward, partly obscuring the fact that the sequence initiated by (2) remains incomplete. We may note that the

		sequence of commands – (2) and (9) – implies the existence of a perspective within the action from which such fragmentary glimpses as the reader receives can be seen to form part of an organized and coherent whole.
(10)	He saw the boat, manned, drop swiftly below the rail, and rushed after her.	The response to (9) is immediate: the cutter is lowered. That it is lowered already "manned" not only implies completion of the sequence initiated in (2) but also draws attention to the fact that the actual "manning" was elided in the narrative, raising the question of when it could have taken place. (The obvious answer is "during" [8].) This sentence also transforms Jim's passive observance into action at last.

The passage neither creates nor sustains the flow of action; rather, the fragmented sequences and the shifts in tone and perspective suggest Jim's own inability to unite all of these elements coherently, until it is too late. The narrative employs paralipsis – defined by Genette as "the omission of one of the constituent elements of a situation in the period that a narrative does generally cover ... the narrative does not skip over a moment of time, as in an ellipsis, but it *sidesteps* a given element" (1980, 51-52, emphasis in the original.) – to distinguish Jim from his peers *for the wrong reason*. By encouraging the simple, misleading opposition – Jim's passivity *versus* the action of the boys – the narrative creates the illusion that only Jim is innocent of action, an impression later contradicted when "Eager listeners crowded round" (8) the hero of the rescue while Jim sits apart lost in self-aggrandizing dreams. Jim's uniqueness thus lies not in his immobility (the effect of the simple opposition) but rather his need to believe something about himself, not just to make excuses for not having acted but to elevate himself above those who have.

The disrupted chronological order interrupts causal analysis and, in doing so, privileges subjective experience above "clock time." For example, the overview (4), that initiates our sequence chronologically, is positioned where its meaning is logically most likely to have become clear to the collective consciousness of the crew. Furthermore, as certain events probably occurred simultaneously – (1) and (3), for instance, or (5) and (7) – their dislocation emphasizes (and anticipates) the confrontation between clock time, in which factual events occur, and psychological time, in which they are experienced and understood, in *Lord Jim*. Jim's romanticism, echoed in the poetic interpolation (8), is contrasted with his duty as a seaman to man the cutter, while his passivity is set against his sudden action, in (10), when it is too late. This double movement is reflected in the pattern it imposes upon our reading of the novel: the degree to which we already know the answers means that we are constantly reading "backwards" in a truth-seeking endeavour. That Jim's failure to respond is occasioned by "awe" rather than fear makes it difficult to forecast what will happen. We are allowed only limited interpretation: we have the fact but not the reason – just as we don't know exactly what Jim saw when the boys manned the boat. The prose is informative but not totally so. The opening chapters of *Lord Jim* reveal the limits of what can be done with a continually shifting focus of perception and create a demand for a "human being" (Marlow), through whom Conrad effects both the mystery surrounding the figure of Jim and, simultaneously, a dispassionate view of his failings. Such ambiguity, inscribed at the level of narration, ensures that the narrative will be ambiguous, its tensions resulting from the coexistence of opposing forces: the reader's desire for certainty, on the one hand, and the impossibility of certainty, on the other.

Micro-structurally, then, the narrative is composed according to a principle of anticipatory gestures that, I shall argue, frustrate the interpretive quests they invite the reader to follow. Examining these fine chains of association in *Lord Jim* reveals that the hero's constant pursuit of an "ideal of conduct" (416) is structurally complemented by the consistency with which the narrative anticipates impending events. But two contrasted impulses are at work within the narrative: it is pre-emptive, often revealing the outcome of events well in advance of their sequential occurrence in the narrative order; and yet, while this tacitly suggests that the tale's meaning will be readily discoverable, it coexists with an opposing tendency to confound this expectation. It is to this aspect of narrative that I shall now turn.

In the trial scene, a simile is employed to describe Jim's state of mind in terms that anticipate his subsequent imprisonment in the Rajah's stockade in Patusan:

> it was like a creature that, finding itself imprisoned within an enclosure of high stakes, dashes round and round, distracted in the night, trying to find a weak spot, a crevice, a place to scale [...] (31).

This image, which exists purely for the reader's benefit (since Jim doesn't see himself in these terms), is consistent with the tenor of the opening chapters in providing information that affords the reader a privileged (although, as yet, unappreciated) perspective of events to follow. Furthermore, in a narrative where the concreteness of Patusan – and, by extension, Jim's successes there – is at best equivocal, the subsequent realization of this metaphor encourages attention to the interplay between figural language and literal fact. As Genette argues, "Every figure is translatable, and bears its translation, transparently visible, like a watermark, or a palimpsest, beneath its apparent text. Rhetoric is bound up with the duplicity of language" (1982, 50).

Most obviously, realization of the imprisonment-image suggests the coincidence of the worlds of the *Patna* and Patusan. When Jim is *literally* incarcerated in the Rajah's stockade, he is engaged in the allegorical activity of trying to repair a clock "of *New* England make" (252, emphasis added). Interpretations of this incident are manifold: Jim is trying to get the mechanics of civilization going in a world outside it; he is endeavouring to introduce a sense of time, and thus reality, into Patusan, whose imaginary status depends in large part upon its timelessness (a point Marlow makes when leaving: "I had turned away from the picture and was going back to the world where events move, men change" [330]); the incident functions as a colonialist trope, implying that the non-European world exists in timeless stasis and is, by extension, both exotic and unreal; and so on. (One wonders, too, whether a favoured eighteenth-century image of God the watchmaker is being sent up here.) The wider inference that Jim is trying to "repair time" gains from the role watches have played in the life of Stein: it is consistent with Stein's own second chance as a hawker of cheap watches (205), figuratively a provider of time, that he should provide Jim with his fresh start in Patusan.

Various critics have noted how Jim's leap from the stockade serves to reverse his earlier leap from the *Patna*. Tony Tanner's comment is typical: "in this magic world Jim does manage to make a successful leap out of the stockade of facts. His first leap in the other world was a fall, a descent: his second jump is a triumph, an ascent" (1975, 47). Fredric

Jameson suggests an even more complex chain of inference, arguing that Jim's jump from the *Patna* is itself a second chance, giving him "the unexpected opportunity to complete his long-suspended act, and to land in the cutter over which he was poised so many years before" (1981, 263). Over-ingenious though this triple sequence may seem – from the non-jump on the training-ship, to the *Patna* jump, to the jump over the stockade – making the *Patna*-jump the central term of the progression, highlights the disruptive effect upon our interpretation created by Jim's failure to recall actually jumping. The narrative thus leads up to and then looks back upon a moment that is suppressed: "'I had jumped. . .' He checked himself, averted his gaze. . . 'It seems,' he added. ... 'I knew nothing about it till I looked up,' he explained hastily." (111) This suppression raises the question of how we judge someone who is, paradoxically, innocent of the transgression he has committed. It also renders the narrative proleptic and analeptic about a moment it elides, implicitly questioning the figures through which the novel's convergent meaning emerges.

The convergence of the imprisonment image with its literal meaning coexists with an obvious failure to reconcile Jim's literally successful leap from the stockade and his failure to mend the clock. The narrative tendency to realize its figures carries the suggestion that it is revealing the secrets of its own composition. But, as this example shows, at the point of actualizing one figure (the anticipatory imprisonment-image), unambiguous meaning is deferred by the inconsistency within another: the *Patna*-jump remains identified with unrepaired time.

The imprisonment-simile describing Jim's state of mind during the Inquiry constitutes a sign in which the signified (Jim's mental state) is described in terms of a signifier (captivity), but this sign is itself a signifier, signifying Jim's subsequent imprisonment. Interpretation is first promoted through the anticipatory gesture, the image, then frustrated, with its realization. In fact, the realization quickly gives way to paradox and oxymoron as, floundering in the mud immediately after his escape, Jim longs for his recently escaped incarceration:

> He told me that he remembered suddenly the courtyard as you remember a place where you had been very happy years ago. He longed – so he said – to be back there again, mending the clock. Mending the clock – that was the idea. (254)

Jim's desire undermines the connection between "mending time" and successfully leaping from the stockade. Substituting the metaphor's literal meaning for its figurative meaning does not engender synthesis, rather it threatens the propositions it had encouraged earlier. So, when Marlow subverts the idea of Jim's freedom *outside* the stockade – telling us that "Jim the leader was a captive in every sense" (262) and that "he was imprisoned within the very freedom of his power" (283) – he uses at the end of a chain of meaning that began with metaphor the antithetical figure of oxymoron. That these figures constitute poles on the same axis, as it were, suggests that meaning in *Lord Jim* lies in the tension between, rather than the reconciliation of, resemblance and difference. Conrad's view of narrative plurality is well known. For instance, in his letter of 14 May 1918 to Barrett H. Clark, he wrote:

> a work of art is very seldom limited to one exclusive meaning and not necessarily tending to a definite conclusion. And this for the reason that the nearer it approaches art, the more it acquires a symbolic character.
> (Jean-Aubry 1927, II:205)

The persistent use of anticipatory images in *Lord Jim* invite us to observe how the narrative makes its meaning, only to suspend our interpretation of this meaning between literal and figural readings, neither of which can be refused. In a Freudian sense, the anticipatory gestures are repetitions that are going through different transformations, creating a "neurotic" text.

I have considered the structural use of anticipatory gestures in *Lord Jim* and how these gestures predict the tale and then frustrate themselves when they are followed through. Jim's experiences are predicated upon and anticipated by the experiences of others in the novel, rendering this a self-generating text. To consider a further dimension of this, I shall now turn to the dreams of heroism upon which Jim's self-ideal is founded and consider their anticipatory quality.

Where do Jim's dreams of maritime heroism come from? His decision to go to sea in the first place is described thus: "after a course of light holiday literature his vocation for the sea had declared itself" (5). This literature invests Jim with a self-ideal that manifests itself in the training-ship, first, in the "contempt" for his fellows born of the belief that he is "a man destined to shine in the midst of dangers," and, second, and more fully, in the vision of himself:

saving people from sinking ships, cutting away masts in a hurricane, swimming through the surf with a line; or as a lonely castaway, barefooted and half naked, walking on uncovered reefs in search of shell-fish to stave off starvation. He confronted savages on tropical shores, quelled mutinies on the high seas, and in a small boat upon the ocean kept up the hearts of despairing men – always an example of devotion to duty, and as unflinching as a hero in a book. (6)

Of course, these self-aggrandizing dreams are undercut by Jim's failure to react to the call to duty that immediately follows, but they persist. On the *Patna*, for example, we learn that Jim's thoughts are "full of valorous deeds: he loved these dreams and the success of his imaginary achievements" (20), while he looks down on the rest of the crew because "those men did not belong to the world of heroic adventure" (24).

However unreal Jim's adventure-story dreams may seem, perhaps their most surprising aspect is the fact that they *are* realized by others in the narrative. For example, Brown's Solomon Islander does swim through the surf with a line (355), Bob Stanton does attempt to save people on the sinking *Sephora* (149-51), "Big Brierly" has saved lives at sea (57), Gentleman Brown's is "a harrowing and desperate story" that includes sustaining his crew, short of food and water (356). But these acts are denuded of romance when they *are* attempted or performed in the narrative by others. For instance, Bob Stanton's death is described serio-comically, while Brown and his crew are renegades. This suggests that heroism, at least in the untarnished sense that Jim understands it, is a fiction. Thus, we might argue that when Marlow assures us that Jim would be "loved, trusted, admired, with a legend of strength and prowess forming round his name as though he had been the stuff of a hero" (175), he proclaims Jim's heroism after heroism itself has been debunked. Defining this reference as a further instance of frustrated anticipatory gesture gains when we remember that it is positioned *after* Marlow's comments about "the *fanciful* realm of recklessly heroic aspirations" and "the *impossible* world of romantic achievements" (83, emphases added).[4]

---

[4] A variant on this anticipatory technique was suggested to me when I was fortunate enough to read Rodie Sudbery's (unpublished) Ph.D. thesis on suicide in Conrad: in so far as Jim bases his own dreams on other models of conduct, Brierly, with his "excellence of ... seamanship and ... indomitable pluck" and the fact that he is "second to none" and had "always done his duty" (58, 62), constitutes a further model. Yet Brierly commits suicide (58-59), so, if we associate Jim with such paragons of

It has become something of a critical commonplace to argue that Modernist literary texts contain and self-consciously reveal their processes of composition, that they become, in fact, texts about writing texts. The fact that the "sea-life of light literature" (6) *does* find such echoes in *Lord Jim* suggests, in part at least, that the narrative contains within it the seeds of its own conception, and invites consideration of anticipatory gestures generally. But the fact that characters in the novel *do* perform these storybook feats confuses the narrative level at which characters like Brierly and Jim exist with that at which Jim's "fictional" models exist.

Consider some of the problems. Embedding the (intradiegetic) Marlow narrative within the (extradiegetic) frame narration creates an initial shift in narrative levels. Then, within this, Jim becomes the subject of speculation and tales told by others about him. The juxtaposition of these narrative levels threatens the coherence of the picture of Jim: it is a collage composed of narratives of varying degrees of authority. Like Marlow, we have only "fragmentary" information, of differing degrees of veracity, out of which "to make an intelligible picture" (343). Added to this, Jim's career as seaman is driven by *fictions* about sealife, the fiction-within-fiction of his light holiday literature. But these fictions are realized, creating further slippage between narrative levels, and reminding one of how the governess's reading in James's *The Turn of the Screw* renders her experiences at Bly ambivalent. In this vein, Jim's Patusan experiences not only afford a wish-fulfilment of his dreams inspired by the nineteenth-century adventure-story tradition but also carry echoes of the generic parodies we find in novels like *Northanger Abbey*, that invite consideration of the boundary between real and fictional worlds. The degree to which the narrative in *Lord Jim* calls into question its own fictionality is extensive: Jim himself describes Stein's present of the pistols as being "like something you read of in books" (233-34) and compares Doramin's family to "people in a book" (260). The presentation of Patusan itself threatens the "reality" of the text: first, because of its status as a place where "dreams come true"; secondly, because it is repeatedly described as imaginary, as, for instance, when Marlow connects it with "pure exercises of imagination" (282); and, thirdly, because moral

---

behaviour, then we can also see his suicide as being anticipated in the text. (Of course, this further underscores the anticipation of Jim's suicide that is generated by the symbolic substitution of Jim for Stein's dead butterfly.)

values there seem somehow inconsistent with those in the preceding narrative – one thinks, for instance, of how the death of Sherif Ali's followers during the storming of his fort is presented inconsequentially.

In current jargon, *Lord Jim*'s blurring of the boundary between these different fictional "worlds" renders it "post-modern" in the sense that it generates ontological confusion as to which of these worlds is the real one. The most obvious example of this is found at the macro-structural level in the juxtaposition of the *Patna* and Patusan worlds, where the latter is presented as less real than the former. By contrast with the psychological intensity and implied veracity of Jim's *Patna* ordeal, Patusan's reality (and thus the reality of Jim's rehabilitation itself) is repeatedly rendered questionable, through such descriptions of it as being "situated internally" (238), its inhabitants as "people in a book" (260), the moonshine by which it is characteristically viewed, the claim that, in going there, Jim "left his *earthly* failings behind him" (218, emphasis added), and the legends and rumours that invest Jim with unbelievable powers. (In fact, this latter provides an instance of fiction doubly generating fiction, since Jim's investiture carries echoes of Alfred Russel Wallace's account of James Brooke, for which Wallace himself employed fictional tropes.) But the implications of this for the reader are profound: the narrative anticipates a conclusion only to return us to realms of fiction, reminding us that we are reading a novel, possibly even reinforcing our sense of security by insulating us against the real life implications of the story. The structure reminds one of a Klein bottle, that frustrates completion by turning in upon itself. Interpretively, the anticipation that is created crosses from one fictional world (that of the *Patna*) to another (Patusan), and then this second fictional world is presented as unreal. This narrative layering extends to "the story of [Jim's] love" (275) which is itself presented in terms of another fictional text with "knight and maiden meeting to exchange vows amongst haunted ruins" (312) – another ur-text, another unreality.

Patusan's presentation is topsy-turvy: it includes contradiction, paradox, oxymoron, and synaesthesia. For instance, we view the "*remnants* of [Sherif Ali's] *impregnable* camp" (263); Tamb' Itam is a jailer ready to die for his captive (284); Jewel is a mixture of "shyness and audacity" (282); her voice is "as quiet ... as her white half-lost figure" (312); Jim displays "a contemptuous tenderness" (248). Yet it is here, in this story-book place, that, Marlow assures us, Jim achieves "greatness as genuine as any man ever achieved" (244). The reader is ultimately left with only a choice of fictions (rather than "nightmares") about Jim – fictions that extend to include the codes of seamanship and heroism themselves.

Critics such as J. Hillis Miller have read the novel in terms of its repetitions, repetitions that I have claimed constitute part of its frustrated anticipatory pattern. These repetitions extend to characters beyond Jim, linking their "realities," often in very subtle ways. Thus Brown's anger at his entrapment in Patusan reduces to being outnumbered "two hundred to one" (371), exactly the same proportion of *Patna* passengers to crew survivors while, taking leave of Brown, Jim stands "on the very spot where for the first time he put his foot on Patusan shore" (398). Such emphasis on structural precision coexists with the narrative's corresponding tendency to mystify, affording an almost derisory promise of order and coherence for, like Marlow, we are left with "that doubt which is the inseparable part of our knowledge" (221) of Jim. But then *Lord Jim* might be said to make interpretation a conscious issue in Marlow's curious claim that "the power of sentences has nothing to do with their sense or the logic of their construction" (75).[5] How words convey meaning is thus left undefined, rendering the process of communication in the novel comparable both to the reader's quest for certainty in a narrative whose strategies eschew certainty, and to the "romantic" (212) Jim's pursuit of an ideal of conduct in an imperfect world. This pursuit, that is perhaps designed to mirror the reading process itself, recalls the plight of Keats's "Bold Lover" in "Ode on a Grecian Urn":

> never, never canst thou kiss,
> Though winning near the goal – yet, do not grieve;
> She cannot fade, though thou hast not thy bliss,
> For ever wilt thou love, and she be fair!

---

[5] For Conrad, then, the power of sentences would appear to depend upon the charisma of the speaker, as he writes in *Nostromo*: "The value of a sentence is in the personality which utters it" (181).

WORKS CITED

Barthes, Roland. "Introduction to the Structural Analysis of Narratives." In *Image, Music, Text*, edited and translated by Stephen Heath, 79-124. New York: Hill and Wang, 1977.
Culler, Jonathan. *Structuralist Poetics*. London: Routledge & Kegan Paul, 1975.
Genette, Gérard. *Figures of Literary Discourse*. Translated by Alan Sheridan. New York: Columbia University Press, 1982.
———. *Narrative Discourse*. Translated by Jane E. Lewin. Oxford: Blackwell, 1980.
Jameson, Fredric. *The Political Unconscious: Narrative as a Socially Symbolic Act*. London: Methuen, 1981.
Jean-Aubry, G., ed. *Joseph Conrad: Life & Letters*. 2 vols. London: Heinemann, 1927.
Kermode, Frank. *Essays on Fiction: 1971-82*. London: Routledge & Kegan Paul, 1983.
Leavis, F. R. *The Great Tradition: George Eliot, Henry James, Joseph Conrad*. London: Chatto & Windus, 1948.
Miller, J. Hillis. *Fiction and Repetition*. Oxford: Blackwell, 1982.
Stape, J. H. "Serialization." In *The Oxford Reader's Companion to Conrad*, edited by Owen Knowles and Gene M. Moore, 339. Oxford: Oxford University Press, 2000.
Sudbery, Rodie. "Stormie Seas: A study of the part played by suicide in the life and work of Joseph Conrad." Ph.D. thesis, University of York, 2000.
Tanner, Tony. *Conrad: Lord Jim* [Studies in English Literature No. 12]. London: Edward Arnold, 1975.

READING AS HOMECOMING:

EXPATRIATION AS A CRITICAL DISCOURSE IN *LORD JIM*

Ludmilla Voitkovska
University of Saskatchewan

... like every inspired raconteur Conrad modified his stories subtly, so as to get in sympathy with his listener.   (Ford Madox Ford)

In Ford's recollection of Conrad's storytelling strategies, he singles out Conrad's sensitivity to the cultural background of his listeners. Told to Ford alone, the story afterwards used in *Romance* was "thinner, less underlined, more of a business-like subject for treatment," while the same story told to a French woman who was also a novelist was "much livelier, much more punctuated with gestures and laughs – much more *pimenté*; in fact, the story of a sailor's *bonne fortune*" (1924, 73). Conrad's sensitivity to his reader's cultural background, which, by virtue of his expatriate condition was always different from his own, rises to the level of extreme anxiety when the writer, in the absence of physical contact with the actual reader, knows that he has no extra-textual means of bridging or compressing the cultural distance. Conrad's extraordinary concerns about his relationships with a readership he adopted seem justified as one analyses critical responses to the political orientation of the characters in *Lord Jim*.

Indeed, depending on a critic's cultural background, Marlow becomes an imperialist nationalist, a challenge to British colonialism, or a mirror of the author's desire to establish a distance between himself and English culture. Postcolonial criticism represents Marlow's narrative as "a secular epiphany which conflates personal salvation with nationalism, and blurs the distinction between knightly quest and mercantile imperialism" (Fincham 1998, 68), but tends to ignore Conrad's expatriate condition even though one of the major premises of this critical approach is to reveal the social and historical contexts of utterances.[1] In turn, Polish Conradians,

---

[1] By ignoring these contexts postcolonial criticism unwittingly banishes the author from his own narrative and thus supports Barthes's "death of the author" claim that "it

who tend to be conscious of authorial presence in Conrad's fiction, view Marlow as the embodiment of what Conrad would have wished to be had he been completely anglicized. Zdzisław Najder maintains that Conrad does not quite identify himself with Marlow, either emotionally or intellectually, since complete assimilation is, in principle, not possible; the character of Marlow allows Conrad to entertain the sense of belonging to England "by proxy, at the same time maintaining a distance such as one has toward a creation of one's imagination" (1983b, 231). British criticism establishes a still greater tension between Marlow and Conrad. For instance, Andrzej Gasiorek feels that *Lord Jim* "not only ironizes [Marlow] but also asks more searching questions about the imperial enterprise than he ever could. ... The distance between Marlow and Conrad becomes apparent when one considers that the latter's similar involvement in the British merchant navy did not blind him to imperialism's sordid and self-serving aspects" (1998, 109). Gasiorek goes so far as to maintain that Marlow's character resists interpretation since the reader of *Lord Jim* is left "neither with a clear view of Jim nor with a full understanding of Marlow," but is instead offered "a plethora of competing perspectives that remain mutually incommensurable" (107-8). Is there, however, a substantive explanation behind Marlow's elusive cultural identity that depends neither on a reader's ethno-cultural background nor on the text's formal characteristics?

Lord Jim's structural complexity demands attention to a close relationship between narration, interpretation, and reading. Conrad's heightened sensitivity to the role of the reader in the process of creating the text's meaning, as well as to the place of the author in the narrative, is essentially a function of his expatriation. Conrad's exilic condition severed him from the audience he would have been connected with on the instinctual level of the parent culture. Like that of Jim, " a seaman in exile from the sea" (4), his narrative reads like "the aimless startled cry of a solitary man confronted by his fate" (340). Thrown into a foreign and, at times, unsympathetic society with a language that needed to be mastered, Conrad

---

is the language which speaks, not the author; to write is, through a prerequisite impersonality (not at all to be confused with the castrating objectivity of the realist novelist), to reach that point where only the language acts, 'performs,' and not 'me'" (1977, 143). However, even if one assumes that the author makes no significant contribution to his or her own narrative, one has to recognize that, in the process of writing, the first language performs differently from an acquired one.

no doubt had difficulties finding his audience. Could the adopted audience help him in his creative work? In what ways could the specific modes of reception influence literary production? Who should be his implied, and, most importantly, his ideal reader? Conrad's search for acceptance is coloured by additional anxieties that stem from his specific condition as a literary outsider in the relatively homogenous linguistic culture of late nineteenth- and early twentieth-century Britain.

Conrad's anxiety of literary identity fuelled his interest in the author-text-reader paradigm that is partly responsible for the novel's complex narrative structure. Introducing multiple readers of Jim's story of his jump (Marlow, Brierly, the Court of Inquiry, Stein, the French Lieutenant, Chester), Conrad investigates the relationship between the author of what is essentially an expatriate narrative, the narrative itself, and its various readers with their culturally and ideologically specific responses. Therefore, Conrad's critical discourse in *Lord Jim* has two essential components: one of them – Jim's attempts to tell his story to Marlow – is the discussion of an author-text paradigm by recreating the process of reworking a system of mental representation of lived experience into a specifically literary discourse. Thus, Jim's jump, the author's objective correlative, allows Conrad to translate the autobiographical experience of expatriation and its repercussions into the narrative. The second component of Conrad's critical discourse – the introduction of multiple readers of the same episode – reconstructs the relationship between the reader and the text by introducing reading as transactional interpretation. This view of the reader-text relationship anticipates the cornerstone principles of reader-response theory.

Conrad inverts an established creative writing/criticism hierarchy by foregrounding the figure of Marlow the reader. This allows him to enact and observe the levels of individual reading, introducing an essentially phenomenological dimension into the critical discourse. Through the multiple readers of Jim's narrative, Conrad examines a literary text as the process of signification materialized only in the process of reading. The reader makes implicit connections, fills in gaps, draws inferences, and tests out hunches; to do this means drawing on a tacit knowledge of the world in general, which the reader knows mainly through his or her culture, and of literary conventions in particular. The narrational structure of *Lord Jim*, emphasising both the oral mode of telling the story and representing multiple levels of readings of the same story, stems from the author's own exilic displacement which itself can be seen to foreground human communication and accentuate its importance. The expatriate writer's archetypal linguistic and cultural alienation translates into an attempt to test readers of various cultural and ideological backgrounds and investigate how their interaction with the story changes its meaning. Conrad restates the importance of the reader's self-identification in the novel's epigraph: "It is certain my conviction gains infinitely the moment another soul will believe in it."

Wolfgang Iser argues that a literary work has two poles, the artistic and the esthetic: "the artistic refers to the text created by the author, and the esthetic to the realization accomplished by the reader" (1989, 1219). In *Lord Jim*, these two poles are provided by Jim the author and Marlow the reader. Indeed, Marlow relates several characters' responses to Jim's jump: the French Lieutenant, Brierly, Stein, and the Court of Inquiry not only make pronouncements about the story, but are also interacting with its author, each forming the *gestalt* of a literary text. Jim's jump, which prevents him from ever going home, marks his archetypal exilic leap from one set of social conventions to another and becomes the most traumatic experience of his life; it both shapes his future and drives his narrative. His story conveys the expatriate trauma of severing ties with familiar socio-cultural and geographic environment and of encountering an alien milieu. Jim's attempts to tell Marlow his version of the story as well as Marlow's, Stein's, Brierly's, and the French Lieutenant's comments on Jim's situation mirror both the experience of writing an expatriate narrative and Conrad's search for an ideal reader as he attempts to enact the culturally specific responses of different kinds of readers to what is essentially an expatriate narrative.

This essay will now examine the levels of reading enacted through various characters' culturally and ideologically coloured responses to Jim's jump, which constitutes the centre of Conrad's critical discourse within the writer/reader paradigm in the context of the author's complex cultural situation as an expatriate writer. The novel thus becomes for Conrad a major field where critical observations about the impact of expatriation on writing can be simultaneously enacted and observed.

Conrad's attempt at the psychoanalytic study of readers anticipates Norman Holland's suggestion that "interpretation is a function of identity" (1980, 123). The Court of Inquiry's reading of Jim's story from the perspective of facts thematizes the role of the ideologically rigid reader-accuser who prosecutes, judges, and requires unconditional devotion to the beliefs of the parent culture. Reduced to the question-and-answer format required by the context of the telling, the Court's version of the jump is a narrative autocratically guided by the reader. The court of his country – transplanted to an alien environment – creates a hostile environment in which the question-and-answer arrangement does not allow Jim to tell the story the way he feels it should be told, as "the terribly distinct questions that extorted his answers seemed to shape themselves in anguish and pain within his breast – came to him poignant and silent like the terrible questioning of one's conscience" (8). Trapped by the power of the reader's ideological expectations, Jim cannot tell the story he wishes to tell. As the author of an expatriate narrative, Jim is caught up in a pattern of self-justification that becomes a crucial force driving his narrative.[2] Moreover, the negative impact of the rigid ideologically-oriented reader on the writer's creativity becomes obvious from Marlow's description of the hearing's stifling influence on Jim:

> For days, for many days, he had spoken to no one, but had held silent, incoherent, and endless converse with himself, like a prisoner alone in his cell or like a wayfarer lost in a wilderness. ... he doubted whether he would ever again speak out as long as he lived. The sound of his own truthful statements confirmed his deliberate opinion that speech was of no use for him any longer. (33)

The Court of Inquiry – the dictatorial reader representing the establishment of the country Jim left behind as the result of his jump – is essentially the reader from the parent culture who represents and generates mainstream ideologies. By imposing the most rigid expectations on the expatriate writer's thematic choices, this reader also paralyses his creativity. The Inquiry's version of the story of Jim's jump mirrors Conrad's apprehension of the Polish reader's judgement of his work from a political perspective.[3] Indeed, the reason the official version of the jump fails to

---

[2] Hampson interprets Jim's relationship with his past in terms of identity crisis as "the lesion between his identity-for-self and his identity-for-the-other" (1992, 128). However, this interpretation does not explain the reasons behind Jim's identity crisis; one cannot reveal them without resorting to the exilic paradigm.

[3] The attitude towards emigration in Poland had changed throughout the nineteenth century, and by the turn of the century some prominent voices spoke strongly against the emigration of talent. One such voice was that of Eliza Orzeszkowa who, in her

convey what Jim considers essential to his story in that the Inquiry aims at facts: "They wanted facts. Facts! They demanded facts from him, as if facts could explain anything!" (29). Facts, according to Marlow, do not tell the story since they fail to explain the truth, even though they seem to be a truthful representation of reality. Jim is anxious to convey another reality, "a directing spirit of perdition that dwelt within, like a malevolent soul in a detestable body " (31). This metaphysical reality is no less important than the reality of facts, but is completely lost in a narrative relying exclusively on facts, however "visible, tangible, open to the senses" (30) they might be. Thus, according to Conrad, a story shaped exclusively by the political expectations of a reader from the parent culture fails to convey the storyteller's metaphysical vision of reality, as "you can't expect the constituted authorities to inquire into the state of a man's soul" (56-57). Moreover, politically driven narratives address a limited body of readers sharing broadly similar political views, whereas Marlow, the independent reader not involved in the trial's politics and therefore not guided in his attitude to Jim by the official version of the story, is lost by such narratives. The loss turns out to be considerable, since it is due to Marlow's efforts as the reader and interpreter of Jim's life that the world gets to hear Jim's side of the story. The Court of Inquiry's pragmatic reading, which fails to account for the reasons behind his jump, prevents Jim from establishing a connection with the politically prejudiced reader through a factual narrative.

All émigré stories reflecting the trauma of the leap from one culture to another embrace the basic archetypes of expatriate sensibility. However, even though the text is referential, the imaginary universes that readers construct through their readings are not identical. As Todorov has pointed out, the imaginary universe evoked by the author transmutes into the imaginary universe constructed by the reader (1980, 72). Consequently, the reader's account could differ dramatically from the author's. According to Conrad, literary work is an intended act of the consciousness of the author that is then re-experienced or realized in the consciousness of the reader.

1889 article in the newspaper *Kraj*, accused Conrad of treason: "Creative talent forms the very crown of the tree, the pinnacle of the tower, the life-blood of the nation. And to take away that flower, to remove that pinnacle, to drain away that life-blood from the nation in order to pass it on to the Anglo-Saxons (who anyway lie on the bed of roses) just because they pay better . . . It is even hard to think about it without shame" (Najder, ed., 1983a, 188).

The reader's personal politics are therefore crucial for creating the narrative's meaning. Gerald Prince, a theoretician of reader-response criticism, suggests that "the variety of interpretations to which a narrative text lends itself and the variety of reader responses to that text result in an indefinitely large number of possible readings" (1980, 229-30). Jim's story becomes a set of general directions that the reader actualizes as he brings his own context of beliefs and expectations to assess the narrative's various features.

The French Lieutenant, "one of those steady, reliable men who are raw material of great reputations, one of those uncounted lives that are buried without drums and trumpets under the foundations of monumental successes" (143-44), is the unnamed foreign reader whose imaginary universe is identical with mainstream ideologies. Such a reader, a "mouthpiece of abstract wisdom" (147) who relies heavily on established opinions in constructing the text's meaning, is, as Conrad presents him, condescending, judgemental, indifferent, cynical, and superficial. His reflections about honour suggests that his opinion of Jim's jump has been formed before the actual jump takes place: "The honour . . . . that is real ... And what life may be worth when ... when the honour is gone ... I can offer no opinion – because – monsieur – I know nothing of it" (148). The mainstream ideological reader who thinks he or she has a personal relationship with the transcendental signified is unreliable because such a reader evaluates phenomena as they satisfy the demands of the trade. For this reader, judgement is made before the fact: "Man is born a coward" (147). When his opinion is contested, however, he is ready to withdraw it: "The young man in question might have had the best dispositions" (147-48). His conversation with Marlow, "a thing of empty sounds," has the "blight of futility" (148) and leaves Marlow discouraged about Jim's case. Yet the French Lieutenant does not hesitate to offer his judgements, powerful because of their simplicity: "And so that poor young man ran away along with the others" (145).

West Australian Chester, pearler, wrecker, trader, whaler, "in his own words – anything and everything a man may be at sea, but a pirate" (161), who is also given a chance to offer his opinion on Jim's jump, represents an unsophisticated, pragmatic reader who believes that one should "see things as they are" (162). Equating appearance with reality, he, like the French Lieutenant, offers his opinion with the arrogance of someone who knows everything before the facts are in: "He looked knowingly after Jim. 'Takes it to heart?' he asked, scornfully. 'Very much,' I said. 'Then he's no good,' he opined. 'What's all the to-do about? A bit of ass's skin. That never yet made a man'" (161-62). His machismo leaves no room for looking at Jim's jump other than as an act of cowardice, which is exactly the way Jim, the author, does not want it to be read. Chester, who "made it a practice never to take anything to heart" (162) excludes the author from his reading, since he does not connect with the metaphysical reality of his imaginary world.

Brierly, one of the assessors at the Inquiry's hearings, represents the reader from Jim's parent culture who is in the position to be guided by strong ideological considerations, but who, because of his ability to read beyond appearances, can overcome the limitations of political interpretations. Brierly, who "feels like a fool all the time" (66) during the Inquiry's proceedings, sympathizes with Jim on a deep personal level and expresses such a strong interest in his story that Marlow feels that "at bottom poor Brierly must have been thinking of himself" (66). Brierly's identification with Jim, however, does not mean that Brierly understands Jim's story the way Jim wants it to be understood. At Marlow's suggestion that Jim needs a great deal of courage to face the Court when he could escape with no consequences, Brierly bursts into an emotional soliloquy about courage, suggesting that he disapproves of Jim's jump from a moral and ideological perspective: "'Courage be hanged!' growled Brierly. 'That sort of courage is of no use to keep a man straight, and I don't care a snap for such courage. If you were to say it was a kind of cowardice now – of softness'" (67). Brierly's views of honour and duty are closely intermingled with nationalism: he is disappointed in Jim's intention to face the trial since the publicity is disadvantageous for his profession and country. He seems less affected by the state of Jim's soul than by the attention the case has attracted:

> This infernal publicity is too shocking: there he sits while all these confounded natives, serangs, lascars, quartermasters, are giving evidence that's enough to burn a man to ashes with shame. This is abominable. Why, Marlow, don't you think, don't you feel, that this is abominable; don't you now – come – as a seaman? If he went away all this would stop at once. (67)

Apparently Conrad does not place much hope in such a reader either. For such a reader, identifying with the author of an unconventional story is suicidal: to preserve his own identity, he has to reject Jim's narrative altogether. For Conrad, a person who identifies with ideologies coloured by nationalism is the worst kind of reader, and he does not hesitate to dispatch him as Brierly commits suicide. Considering Conrad's much discussed desire to dissociate himself from partisan politics, such a powerful response to a nationalistic reader is unsurprising.

The figure of Stein, "a wealthy and respected merchant," an adventurer with a "learned appearance" (202), and sometime adviser to a Malay sultan, proves to be significant not only for the development of Jim's life but also for Conrad's investigation of ways of reading. Why does Jim reject Brierly's offer, which would release him from the humiliation of court proceedings, and accept Stein's proposal to go to Patusan? Apparently, in Jim's response to Stein, passionate enthusiasm transcends his ability for linguistic expression: "'Slam the door!' he shouted. 'I've been waiting for that. I'll show yet . . . I'll . . . I'm ready for any confounded thing. . . . I've been dreaming of it . . . Jove! Get out of this. Jove! This is luck at last. . . . You wait. I'll . . .'" (235). The reason behind Jim's strong immediate response to Stein's proposal possibly stems from the fact that Stein, unlike other readers of the jump, proves to be the best reader of Jim's life in immediately identifying the source of Jim's predicament: "He is romantic," Stein says, "and this is very bad" (216). Stein's sympathetic analysis suggests his ability to face, read, and understand emotions; it also means recognizing that Jim's emotional self, the cause of his restlessness, is acceptable. Unlike Marlow, Stein does not think Jim needs to be cured of the disease of romanticism; he believes that the most difficult issue for a romantic is finding one's way in the pragmatic world and retaining one's identity and values. And, indeed, Stein sees that Jim must retain these in order to survive: "strictly speaking, the question is not how to get cured, but how to live" (162).

The combination of Stein's own romanticism, his expatriate background, and his education helps him understand Jim's story. He identifies with Jim as an expatriate: like Jim, who cannot return home to face his father, who will be disappointed to find out about Jim's jump, Stein has "no home to go to" (205). Prior to their meeting, Stein and Jim establish a metaphysical understanding founded on something more immediate and profound than reasonable constructs of verbal communication. Their ability to communicate successfully without having met each other is based on their experience of expatriation. It takes the émigré intellectual who found his place in a foreign milieu to understand the origins of Jim's anxiety. Jim, therefore, finds his ideal reader Stein. Does this mean, though, that, having identified his ideal reader from a foreign milieu, Conrad has freed himself from tensions with the adopted reader? Unfortunately, to be appreciated only by the eccentric figures of cosmopolitan intellectuals, failed revolutionaries, and collectors of beetles does not mean one is successful as a writer as Conrad found in remaining a highly respected but not widely popular writer for the greater part of his career. Conrad's discovery of a cosmopolitan intellectual reader in Stein suggests, in fact, quite a grim prospect: in an adopted culture, an expatriate writer can be appreciated only by the educated elite and the readers whose cultural experiences are complex enough to allow them to transcend the limitations of their own cultures, which includes the English reader as well.

The readers of Jim's jump discussed above never express any doubts about their understanding of the story, but Jim has chosen Marlow as his confidant and stayed with him, even though Marlow repeatedly admits that he does not understand Jim. The answer to this contradiction can be found in Marlow's famous contemplation of home, which is often misinterpreted as an allegiance to English nationalism:

> "I was going home – to that home distant enough for all its hearthstones to be like one hearthstone, by which the humblest of us has the right to sit. We wander in our thousands over the face of the earth, the illustrious and the obscure, earning beyond seas our fame, our money, or only a crust of bread; but it seems to me that for each of us going home must be like going to render an account. We return to face our superiors, our kindred, our friends – those whom we obey, and those whom we love; but even they who have neither, the most free, lonely, irresponsible and bereft of ties – even those for whom home holds no dear face, no familiar voice – even they have to meet the spirit that dwells within the land, under its sky, in its air, in its valleys, and on its rises, in its fields, in its waters and in its trees – a mute friend, judge, and inspirer. ... There are girls we love, the men we look up to, the tenderness, the friendships, the opportunities, the pleasures!" (221-22)

To an unsentimental British critic, this passage sounds like a "commonplace of imperial discourse" (Gasiorek 106); from the postcolonial perspective, this "impassioned rhetoric" reads like a hymn to England reminiscent of nineteenth-century missionary narratives (Fincham 68). Why do critics who do not seem to mind the densely impassioned quality of

Conrad's prose in the first place outrightly dismiss his contemplation of homecoming? First, their readings of this passage displays a profound conflict of sensibilities that has an important cultural dimension. Indeed, coming to the rationalist West, a Polish writer brings all the unchecked and alien passions of the Slavic world that not only find their way into the text in the most bizarrely unpredictable ways, but, to a great extent, also drive the narrative. Similarly, the major point of misunderstanding between Jim and Marlow is Jim's emotionalism, which Marlow can neither embrace nor accept:

> [Jim] tossed his head fearlessly, and I confess that for the first and last time in our acquaintance I perceived myself unexpectedly to be thoroughly sick of him. Why these vapourings? He was stumping about the room flourishing his arm absurdly, and now and then feeling on his breast for the ring under his clothes. Where was the sense of such exaltation in a man appointed to be a trading-clerk, and in a place where there was no trade – at that? Why hurl defiance at the universe? This was not a proper frame of mind to approach any undertaking; an improper frame of mind not only for him, I said, but for any man.   (235-36)

Marlow's negative response to Jim's "improper" emotional outbursts mirror Western critics' response to those of Marlow. Conrad, in fact, feels that he is upsetting the British reader by defying cultural conventions – which discourage a public display of emotions – when he apologizes for it in the middle of Marlow's soliloquy: "All this may seem to you [the English reader] sheer sentimentalism," he says (222). He is right. It does.

The other reason why Marlow's contemplation of home sounds out of key to Conrad's adopted reader is that, trying to read this digression realistically, critics mistake it for Marlow's, and, by association, Conrad's feelings for England. There is no indication, however, that Marlow is referring to England when he talks about the hearthstones of home. Critics, in fact, fill in the gap by reconstructing their own imaginary universes. Since Marlow and Jim are English, what other country can Conrad's character refer to? It is easy to miss Conrad's clue about Jim's – and, correspondingly, Marlow's – un-English origin, which he suggests in the same paragraph: "I do not mean to imply that I figured to myself the spirit of the land uprising above the white cliffs of Dover" (223). Moreover, in his 1917 "Author's Note," Conrad says that Jim is "not a figure of Northern Mists" (ix).

Since Conrad's expatrial displacement disconnects him from both the parent and the adopted culture, he apparently refers to a generalized notion of home devoid of clearly defined cultural and geographical specificity. While talking about home, Marlow persistently returns to the image of the "disembodied, eternal, and unchangeable" spirit of the land, with "its secular right to our fidelity, to our obedience" (222), which suggests that for him home has become an archetypal exilic ideal that, like paradise, can be neither regained nor revisited.

Thus, as Marlow says he cannot go home without having resolved Jim's affairs, he descends to the most profound level of his relationship with Jim: attachment based on sharing the same parent culture:

> "I was about to go home for a time; and it may be I desired, more than I was aware of myself, to dispose of him – to dispose of him, you understand – before I left. I was going home, and he had come to me from there, with his miserable trouble and his shadowy claim, like a man panting under a burden in a mist. I cannot say I had ever seen him distinctly – not even to this day, after I had my last view of him; but it seemed to me that the less I understood the more I was bound to him in the name of that doubt which is the inseparable part of our knowledge."
> (221)

The guilt-trap set by the Court of Inquiry forces Jim's narrative into a pattern of self-justification, and Jim therefore reaches for an empathetic reader able to step outside the conventions of the time, political or otherwise. He desperately reaches for Marlow: "I would like to explain – I would like somebody to understand – somebody – one person at least! You! Why not you?" (81). In response to Jim's call, Marlow is forced "to reveal aspects of himself in order to experience reality different from his own" (Iser 1224). According to Iser, "it is only by leaving behind the familiar world of his own experience that the reader can truly participate in the adventure the literary text offers him" (1224), and thus Marlow, the reader of a life he does not understand and the writer of the story he never fully comprehends, becomes the metaphoric double of the writer who drives the discourse of going against the parent culture's highest norms of fidelity to one's country. Telling the story of his experience of expatriation but unable to convey its essential meaning to the listener, Jim is the metaphoric double of the man who breaks the rules of loyalty to his parent culture. Connected by incomprehensible invisible archetypal bonds and outsiders in the social and literary milieu, these two personae represent the anxiety of the expatriate writer who ventures into the world of creative writing in a foreign country in which, at the outset, he is un-equipped with the necessary cultural and linguistic background.

Even if one is able to make the transition to function adequately or even exceptionally in the daily life of commerce and society, when one attempts to communicate through literature, the chasm of language is apparent. Expatriate linguistic and cultural anxiety about the reader surfaces in the works of other highly successful trans-lingual writers. Vladimir Nabokov openly speaks about his disconnection from his adopted American reader in his 1956 "Afterword" to *Lolita*:

> None of my American friends have read my Russian books and thus every appraisal of my English ones is bound to be out of focus. My private tragedy, which cannot, and indeed should not be anybody's concern, is that I had to abandon my natural idiom, my untrammeled, rich, and infinitely docile Russian tongue for a second-rate brand of English, devoid of any of those apparatuses – the baffling mirror, the velvet backdrop, the implied associations and traditions – which the native illusionist, frac-tails flying, can magically use to transcend the heritage in his own way. (298)

As Nabokov responds to American critics' suggestion that *Lolita* is the record of its author's love affair with the romantic novel, he shifts the eternal argument between the author and the critic towards a culturally specific paradigm. Conrad, who does not seem to be affected by Nabokov's linguistic dilemma as he never wrote fiction in his first language, nevertheless exhibits signs of heightened sensitivity to his ability to communicate with his adopted reader. He made a choice of reader by adopting English as the language of his writing: Conrad chose the English reader as definitely as Jim chose Marlow to tell his story to.[4] Jim grows more desperate as he recognizes that Marlow is his only possible sympathetic reader: "You don't know what it is for a fellow in my position to be believed – make a clean breast of it to an elder man. It is so difficult – so awfully unfair – so hard to understand" (128). Consequently, Jim's search for understanding becomes the key to his relationship with Marlow.

---

[4] Interpreting the narrative aspect of the relationships between Marlow and Jim, Ambrosini maintains that "the narrator becomes an ideal reader whose reality has been touched by the truth of Jim's illusion" (158).

Marlow is the only transactive reader of Jim's story, which, as far as Conrad is concerned, makes him an ideal reader. Marlow brings his own individual identity into Jim's story, an identity constructed from all his experiences in the world, his ideas, weaknesses, unconscious desires, and expectations. Marlow's identity sends forth the hypothesis, and the text returns answers that, in turn, become incorporated in Marlow's identity. Marlow's reading of Jim's story "is continuously on the move" (Iser 1223), and the relationship between Jim and Marlow around Jim's story is constructed according to the model of a loop, with the reader in some way constructing the text but with the text also acting on the reader.

The tension in the Jim-Marlow relationship reflects the complexity of a relationship between an expatriate writer and his compatriot reader. On one level, Marlow neither accepts nor understands guilt as the essential paradigm of Jim's narrative; however, on another level, he is attracted to him even though he knows that Jim is guilty. Almost despite himself, Marlow is seduced by Jim's charisma and his story, but he is unable to understand it completely owing to their difference in background, experience, and personal sensibility. This dynamic essentially reflects the pattern of Conrad's relationships with his Polish reader. On the one hand, Conrad's language and subject matter made him a stranger to Polish readers who felt that he did not fulfil their expectations: "His later works, which accounted for his fame in England, seemed to us different and more remote. His thoughts and feelings were more English. Our disappointment grew as this writer, forgetting his home country, merged more and more with the English environment, to such a degree that he even began delivering in real earnest inspired speeches on its behalf. In all his works there was no mention of Poland. We were baffled. But none of us suspected that things would be even worse when he remembered Poland" (cited in Najder 1983a, 158). On the other hand, though, while some of Conrad's books failed to appeal to the Polish public, others evinced unexpected depths of response. Jan Perlowski, Conrad's contemporary, wrote that, through his emotions, Conrad "inadvertently belonged to us: he was one of us in a specific way" (cited in Najder 1983a, 158).

Marlow's acceptance of Jim's persona and his narrative mirrors the Polish audience's reaction to *Lord Jim*. During the Nazi occupation (1939-45), *Lord Jim* was being read in Poland, circulated by the partisans to draw courage and endurance from it. The Polish reader, who had to read Conrad in translation, identified with Jim's restless romanticism, emotional spontaneity, and sensitivity to the concept of honour, which is central to the construction of Polish identity. In the introduction to *Lord Jim*, published in Jerusalem and intended for Polish soldiers and officers, the editor Wit Tarnawski asserted that "the Polish reader had no difficulty, contrary to the English reader" in understanding Jim (cited in Morf 1976, 149). The reason behind the novel's success in Poland lies in the Polish reader's identification with Jim, one facilitated by the drama of Polish history of partitions, wars, and invasions that made every Pole a stranger in his or her own country. Polish readers used to say, "Jim is one of us, he is a Pole" (Morf 149). For Conrad, therefore, the deepest understanding of an expatriate text belongs to the open-minded reader from the parent culture for whom reading means descending to the most intimate levels of the self, which inevitably brings the reader and the writer to their shared and familiar cultural environment. Conrad's genius, however, is in the way he transcends his own anxieties and transforms them into a luring mastery over the foreign reader. Part of the reason he is able to do this is because he reaches the reader he does not know on the level of the archetypal imaginary construct called "home."

Works Cited

Ambrosini, Richard. *Conrad's Fiction as Critical Discourse*. Cambridge: Cambridge University Press, 1991.

Barthes, Roland. "The Death of the Author." In *Image, Music, Text*, edited and translated by Stephen Heath, 142-48. New York: Hill and Wang, 1977.

Fincham, Gail. "The Dialogism of *Lord Jim*." In *Conrad and Theory*, edited by Andrew Gibson and Robert Hampson, 58-74. Amsterdam – Atlanta, GA: Rodopi, 1998.

Ford, Ford Madox. *Joseph Conrad. A Personal Remembrance*. London: Duckworth, 1924.

Gasiorek, Andrzej. "'To Season with a Pitch of Romance': Ethics and Politics in *Lord Jim*." *Conrad and Theory*, edited by Andrew Gibson and Robert Hampson, 75-112. Amsterdam – Atlanta, GA: Rodopi, 1998.

Holland, Norman. "Re-covering 'The Purloined Letter': Reading as a Personal Transaction." In *The Reader in the Text*, edited by Susan R.. Suleiman and Inge Crosman, 350-70. Princeton: Princeton University Press, 1980.

Iser, Wolfgang. "The Reading Process: A Phenomenological Approach." In *The Critical Tradition. Classic Texts and Contemporary Trends*, edited by David H. Richter, 1219-32. New York: St. Martin's Press. 1989.

Morf, Gustav. *The Polish Shades and Ghosts of Joseph Conrad*. New York: Astra, 1976.

Nabokov, Vladimir. "On a Book Entitled Lolita." In *Vladimir Nabokov: Novels 1955-1962*, edited by Brian Boyd, 293-98. New York: The Library of America, 1966.

Najder, Zdzisław, ed. *Conrad Under Familial Eyes*, tr. Halina Carroll-Najder. Cambridge: Cambridge University Press, 1983.

———. *Joseph Conrad: A Chronicle*. Cambridge: Cambridge University Press, 1983.

Prince, Gerald. "Notes on the Text as a Reader." In *The Reader in the Text*, edited by Susan R. Suleiman and Inge Crosman, 225-40. Princeton: Princeton University Press, 1980.

Todorov, Tsvetan. "Reading as Construction." In *The Reader in the Text*, edited by Susan R. Suleiman and Inge Crosman, 67-82. Princeton: Princeton University Press, 1980.

"USQUE AD FINEM": *UNDER WESTERN EYES*, *LORD JIM*, AND CONRAD'S RED UNCLE

Andrzej Busza
University of British Columbia

"The victorious are called great; the vanquished – dreamers."
— Franciszek Rawita-Gawroński

The richness and significance of Conrad's Polish background is today a commonplace. Every serious student of Conrad is familiar with his father's, Apollo Korzeniowski's, literary and political careers, as well as the grim pathos of his exile and last days. Taking their cue from Conrad's own autobiographical testimony in his letters and in such texts as the "Author's Note" to *A Personal Record*, scholars have related characteristic aspects of Conrad's sensibility and outlook to "the exalted and dreamy temperament," the "terrible gift of irony and ... gloomy disposition" of his father (*CL2* 247), while literary critics have discerned traces of Apollo's psychological and ideological make-up in various characters – Kurtz of *Heart of Darkness*, José Avellanos of *Nostromo*, Heyst of *Victory*, to mention but three often-cited figures. Or, to take a recent example, John Batchelor has argued in his critical biography that "the post-romantic view of the relationship between the artist, the art and the audience is more likely to be indebted to Apollo Korzeniowski's mid-nineteenth-century post-romantic view of Shakespeare than it is ... to the English romantic tradition" (1994, 6).

Similarly, Tadeusz Bobrowski, the maternal uncle and the other temperamentally and ideologically antithetical coordinate of Conrad's dual family heritage, has received, especially since the appearance of Jocelyn Baines's *Joseph Conrad: A Critical Biography* (1960), considerable attention. Select passages from Bobrowski's letters and memoirs now form a crucial part of the Conradian documentary canon. We have all come to recognize as a key ingredient of Conrad's polyphonic (largely bitonal) discourse the Bobrowski voice: sober, ironic (not without the occasional drop of universal scorn), puncturing illusions, deriding utopianism and all formulas for the betterment of the human condition, and, yet, not only rejecting nihilism but preaching an austere brand of moral pragmatism, hinged on the virtues of duty, work, restraint, self-discipline, and perseverance *usque ad finem*.[1] Critics like Zdzisław Najder, however, have tended to emphasize Bobrowski's dialogic importance and its corollary: the poignant, painful, and deeply unsettling, although in the final effect highly fruitful, tensions generated by the clash between the uncle's rationalist temper and positivist philosophy and the heroic romanticism of Conrad's father.[2] Indeed, the underlying paradigm of much of Conradian drama at the axiological level is a dialogue between these two discourses. In the case of *Lord Jim* this paradigm affects even the form of the narrative, where the focus of interest is shared by Jim the protagonist and Marlow the dramatized narrator.

Materials relating to Ewa Korzeniowska included by Najder in *Conrad Under Familial Eyes* together with Conrad's own few, brief accounts of his far-from-ordinary mother, to my mind, shed more light on Conrad's portrayal of women than feminist speculations developed within the ideological horizon of Anglo-Saxon bourgeois capitalist society.[3] Even individuals whose lives barely, or only indirectly, touched Conrad's, like those of his grand-uncle Nicholas Bobrowski or Prince Roman Sanguszko,

---

[1] In one of his most interesting and famous letters to Conrad, Tadeusz Bobrowski summarized his philosophy of life: "I have gone through a lot, I have suffered over my own fate and the fate of my family and my Nation, and perhaps just because of these sufferings and disappointments I have developed in myself this calm outlook on the problem of life, whose motto, I venture to say, was, is, and will be 'usque and finem.' The devotion to duty interpreted more widely or narrowly, according to circumstances and time – this constitutes my practical creed" (Najder, ed., 1964, 155).

[2] Najder's *Conrad in Perspective: Essays on Art and Fidelity* contains important new essays on Apollo Korzeniowski and Tadeusz Bobrowski. Najder has never liked Tadeusz Bobrowski, and, although he tries hard to present a balanced view of Conrad's uncle, his bias is still evident. See also, his discussion in *Joseph Conrad: A Chronicle* (1983b).

[3] In the "Author's Note" to *A Personal Record*, Conrad writes: "I remember my mother ... dressed in the black of the national mourning worn in defiance of ferocious police regulations. I have also preserved from that particular time the awe of her mysterious gravity which, indeed, was by no means smileless. For I remember her smiles, too. Perhaps for me she could always find a smile. She was young then, certainly not thirty yet. She died four years later in exile" (xii).

because of the memorable role that each plays in a Conrad narrative, have become the objects of (at times perhaps inordinate) scholarly scrutiny.

One portrait in Conrad's family album deserves, in my view, a second, closer look: Stefan Bobrowski, Tadeusz's and Ewa's younger brother, Apollo Korzeniowski's political disciple, and Conrad's politically most radical relative. Of course, Stefan Bobrowski is anything but an unknown figure. He makes a cameo appearance in every Conrad biography, and has acquired an increasingly prominent place in historical narratives on the 1863 Uprising. If Romuald Traugutt (1825-64) is the hero of the Uprising's last act (he was hanged by the Russians in the Warsaw Citadel on 5 August 1864), the tragic protagonist of its initial phase is Stefan Bobrowski.[4]

Let me rehearse briefly the salient facts of this extraordinary young man's short life, his meteoric rise into the arena of national politics, and early violent death. Born in 1840, Stefan Bobrowski, on the death of his father in 1850, came into the care of his older brother, Tadeusz, at almost the same age as his orphaned nephew, Konrad. For two years Stefan was tutored jointly by Tadeusz and his sister Ewa (Conrad's future mother). "My sister and I," writes Tadeusz Bobrowski in his *Memoirs*, "undertook to prepare our brother for school. My sister taught him religion and languages and I gave lessons in classical subjects; he was a good pupil and his education progressed smoothly" (Najder, ed., 1983a, 26).

Tadeusz continues: "He always carried about him a book which absorbed him at the time, and he used to open it whenever possible. He was extremely short-sighted, and in spite of exhortations he insisted on reading with each eye in turn" (26). Stefan then went on to secondary schools, first locally in the Ukraine, then in St. Petersburg. In 1856, when the post-Crimean War "thaw" was at its warmest, Bobrowski enrolled as a student of philosophy at the University of St. Petersburg. He had already some experience of dissident activity from his schooldays in the Ukraine, but in the Imperial capital he increased considerably the scope of his

---

[4] Stefan Bobrowski is the central figure of Jasienica's monograph on the 1863 Uprising, *Dwie drogi*. The leading contemporary historian of the event was Kieniewicz to whose magisterial study *Powstanie styczniowe* as well as later *Warszawa w powstaniu styczniowym* I am indebted. I also consulted Ramotowska's *Narodziny tajemnego państwa polskiego 1859-1862*. Rawita-Gawroński's *Stefan Bobrowski i dyktatura Langiewicza* is an early discussion of Bobrowski's role in the Uprising. For a clear and concise account of the 1863 Uprising in English, see Davies, 1981, 2: 347-68.

political engagement, becoming involved both in the conspiratorial work of Polish democratic groups and the Russian revolutionary underground.

Next, Stefan moved to Kiev, ostensibly to study philology, though, as a matter of fact, he did not even enrol at the university and merely pretended to be a student, appearing, for instance, in academic uniform in group photographs. Indeed, by now he was a full-time clandestine political activist. From the Kiev period dates the episode of the secret press that, via Tadeusz Bobrowski's account in his *Memoirs*, probably contributed to the atmosphere and certain elements of plot in *Under Western Eyes*. According to Tadeusz Bobrowski, whose version of the story diverges in some details from established historical facts, in 1861 Stefan Bobrowski together with a printer from Warsaw named Hoffman set up a secret lithographic press on the premises of a monastery in Kiev. However, before the press was able to develop its activities fully, Hoffman was suddenly arrested and Bobrowski had to flee the country. The discovery of the press and the conspiratorial cell was the work of an informer who, Tadeusz Bobrowski narrates, "having been caught in Warsaw at revolutionary practices, agreed to undertake spying. Since he could not work in Warsaw, where he was known, he was sent to Kiev to discover the secret lithographic press that had been causing trouble to the police for some time. In Warsaw he had been a student, and so in Kiev he also mixed with students, pretending to be one himself" (2: 466).[5]

The parallels between this informer (in Tadeusz Bobrowski's account) and Razumov, the protagonist of *Under Western Eyes*, are, to say the least, intriguing. There are moreover points of similarity between Stefan Bobrowski's behaviour and that of Haldin. One of the precautions that Bobrowski took, before starting work on the secret press, was to change his lodgings. Haldin also leaves his usual residence some time before the attempt on Mr. de P—'s life. After Hoffman's arrest, Bobrowski hid in the rooms of a fellow student, who was trusted by the authorities on account of his political views. When the watchfulness of the police abated, he escaped from Kiev by sledge, as Haldin plans to do in Conrad's novel. Finally, it is worth noting that Tadeusz (despite his strong disapproval of dissident activities) materially helped his brother to elude the police.

---

[5] Translations from the Polish are my own unless otherwise indicated.

From the historical point of view the most important period of Stefan Bobrowski's life was the first three months of 1863 (the Uprising began on 22 January), when on his return from France he was first appointed to the Central National Committee and then shortly afterwards assumed the responsibilities of Commander of the City of Warsaw. For a while, this barely twenty-two-year-old man from the provinces was, in effect, the leader of the whole insurgent movement. Tellingly, Tadeusz Bobrowski in his 900-page *Memoirs* devotes a single paragraph to this phase of his younger brother's life. Moreover, he stresses Stefan's moderating influence on the leaders of the insurrection. Stefan's influence "on the National Government," writes Tadeusz, "was resolute and humanitarian, as even Russian historians of the period admit. As long as he was a member of the government, he restrained it from terrorist and Jacobin practices!" (2: 472).

The circumstances of Stefan's death receive more typical anecdotal treatment in the *Memoirs*. Admitting gaps and the lack of certainty in his knowledge of the facts, Tadeusz loyally tries to present his brother's conduct (from his point of view) in the best possible light – although it must be remembered (as I have already indicated) that he differed in significant ways with him on ideological and political grounds. Although both brothers agreed on the need for social reforms and, in particular, for the abolition of serfdom, Tadeusz favoured a gradual, pragmatically conceived process, while the younger brother together with other "ultra-democrats" dreamed of an immediate, revolutionary transformation of society. Similarly, while both brothers were, in the final analysis, as deeply and sincerely committed to the ideal of national independence for Poland, Stefan with Apollo Korzeniowski and the "Reds" believed that this goal could be achieved only through armed confrontation with Russia, whereas Tadeusz rejected the idea of armed conflict as impractical given the extreme disproportion of military forces as well as the inopportuneness of the general political situation. In his overview of his brother's personality, Tadeusz writes: "He knew me and my views too well not to realize that if I heard about his revolutionary activities I would try to discourage him. This was probably why he never confided in me on the subject" (Najder, ed., 1983a, 73).

An element of mystery continues to hang over the final act of Stefan Bobrowski's tragic life. The historical context of the events, characterizing the second phase of the Uprising, was the questioning of the nature of the government of the newly and suddenly created counter-state. Bobrowski, together with the more radical "Reds," vigorously resisted abandoning a democratic leadership in favour of some form of dictatorship linked to military prestige and power. The "Whites," as well as some of the moderate "Reds" such as Agaton Giller (a journalist and, like Stefan Bobrowski, a member of the National Central Committee), arguing in terms of efficiency and fearing excessive radicalism particularly in the area of social policy, preferred the dictatorial option. In the version of the events presented by Tadeusz Bobrowski and believed by many historians, Stefan became the victim of a "White" plot aimed at eliminating an awkward opponent. Stefan's integrity and political straight-forwardness as well as his impetuousness and aristocratic sensibility were effectively exploited by a certain Count Adam Grabowski, a man of seedy reputation and a willing pawn of the "White" faction. When Bobrowski refused to shake Grabowski's proffered hand during a meeting in Cracow, the latter challenged him to a duel. At first Bobrowski declined to accept in view of his official function and the exigencies of the wider political situation, as well as the lack of proof that his behaviour was unjustified, but the ruling of a "court of honour"[6] stacked with "White" supporters made him change his mind. Although Bobrowski knew that he could not come out of the duel alive, his sense of honour prevented him from ignoring the court's ruling. The odds were exceptionally uneven: Bobrowski was very short-sighted, and Grabowski was a well-known marksman and duellist. The duel took place on 12 April 1863 near Rawicz in western Poland. Stefan Bobrowski was shot straight through the heart. Tadeusz Bobrowski gives the assassination plot theory a twist of his own: "It is my conviction that, having lost faith in the cause he had embraced [literally, "wedded"] his mind was too alert and realistic to harbour illusions – he no longer wished to live and preferred to die by another's hand than by his own" (2: 476).[7]

One is tempted to continue Tadeusz Bobrowski's elegiac reflection by putting into his mouth some phrases from the end of *Lord Jim*: "And

---

[6] The "court of honour" was a court or tribunal that determined questions concerning the laws and principles of honour and ruled on them in particular cases. It was clearly the successor of medieval courts of chivalry. In *Lord Jim,* Jim, Marlow, who refers to "the honour of the craft" (46), and Brierly all seem to regard the *Patna* Inquiry as a kind of court of honour rather than a professional tribunal concerned simply revoking a certificate.

[7] It is possible that Stefan's fatal duel suggested to Tadeusz Bobrowski the story that he and later Conrad himself used to cover up Conrad's attempted suicide in 1878.

that's the end. He passes away under a cloud, inscrutable at heart, forgotten, unforgiven, and excessively romantic." Responding to "the call of his exalted egoism," he goes away "to celebrate his pitiless wedding with a shadowy ideal of conduct" (416). When chaos returns to Patusan and the edifice of social order, security, and trust, "the work of his hands, had fallen in ruins upon his head" (408), Jim (like Stefan Bobrowski near Rawicz) comes forward unflinchingly to meet certain death. Moreover, the meaning of both deaths remains obscure: having asked Jewel for forgiveness, Jim leaves the girl to lead "a sort of soundless, inert life" (416), while Bobrowski before the fatal duel entrusted to his second a letter to his mother and family in which he asked them to forgive "this last painful blow" (2: 476).[8] The ambiguities of Tadeusz Bobrowski's judgement on his younger brother's life and death seem to have been carried over into the open ending of Conrad's great and, in some respects, his most personal novel.

---

[8] This letter reached his mother only ten years later. It was brought by a stranger in a parcel that also contained Stefan's bloodstained shirt and a lock of his hair.

Works Cited

Baines, Jocelyn. *Joseph Conrad: A Critical Biography*. London: Weidenfeld and Nicholson, 1960.
Batchelor, John. *The Life of Joseph Conrad: A Critical Biography*. Oxford: Blackwell, 1994.
Bobrowski, Tadeusz. *Pamiętnik mojego życia*. Ed. Stefan Kieniewicz. 2 vols. Warsaw: Państwowy Instytut Wydawniczy, 1979.
Busza, Andrzej. "Conrad's Polish Literary Background and Some Illustrations of the Influence of Polish Literature on His Work." *Antemurale* 10 (1966): 109-255.
Davies, Norman. *God's Playground: A History of Poland*. 2 vols. Oxford: Clarendon Press, 1981.
Jasienica, Pawel. *Dwie drogi* [The Two Ways]. Warsaw: Państwowy Instytut Wydawniczy, 1988.
Kieniewicz, Stefan. *Powstanie styczniowe* [The January Uprising]. Warsaw: Państwowe Wydawnictwo Naukowe, 1972.
———. *Warszawa w powstaniu styczniowym* [Warsaw in the January Uprising]. Warsaw: Wiedza Powszechna, 1983
Najder, Zdzisław. *Conrad in Perspective: Essays on Art and Fidelity*. Cambridge: Cambridge University Press, 1997.
———, ed. *Conrad's Polish Background: Letters to and from Polish Friends*. Translated by Halina Carroll. London: Oxford University Press, 1964.
———, ed. *Conrad Under Familial Eyes*. Cambridge: Cambridge University Press, 1983.
———. *Joseph Conrad: A Chronicle*. Translated by Halina Carroll-Najder. New Brunswick, NJ: Rutgers University Press, 1983.
Ramotowska, Franciszka. *Narodziny tajemnego państwa polskiego 1859-1862* [The Birth of the Polish Clandestine State, 1859-1862]. Warsaw: Państwowe Wydawnictwo Naukowe, 1990.
Rawita-Gawroński, Franciszek. *Stefan Bobrowski i dyktatura Langiewicza w roku 1863* [Stefan Bobrowski and the Dictatorship of Langiewicz in the Year 1863]. Warsaw: Gebethner i Wolff, 1914.

This is a revised and expanded version of an article that appeared in The Bulletin of the Polish Institute of Arts and Sciences in Canada *14 (1997): 22-25.*

LOUIS BECKE'S GENTLEMEN PIRATES AND *LORD JIM*

J. H. Stape
Vancouver, British Columbia

The search for real-life sources on which some of the incidents and characters of *Lord Jim* were based has a long and distinguished history in Conrad scholarship. Conrad's suggestion in his 1917 "Author's Note" that Jim himself was to some extent derived from an actual figure glimpsed in "the commonplace surroundings of an Eastern roadstead" (ix) has partly determined these efforts.

John D. Gordan systematically took up the tantalizing challenge of identification in his *Joseph Conrad: The Making of a Novelist* (1940), and Norman Sherry energetically followed in his indefatigably researched *Conrad's Eastern World* (1966), going considerably further than Gordan both in his search for real-life sources and in ferreting out the debts Conrad owed to his reading.[1] All annotated editions of Conrad's Malay fiction draw heavily on this body of work, although the wide range of Conrad's experience and reading has necessarily left open the possibility of the rare nugget here and there awaiting discovery. The sources for Gentleman Brown have thus far largely remained where Gordan and Sherry left them.[2] Finding "nothing really convincing" (354) in the careers of Captains "Bully" Hayes and Ben Pease as parallels,[3] Gordan speculates that "Conrad may have picked up the facts he gave in the story of Gentleman Brown

---

[1] As well as providing new information about Conrad's use of real-life geographical sources, Van Marle and Lefranc offer a useful and carefully balanced assessment of Sherry's methods and identifications.

[2] Browne has not very convincingly suggested a real-life basis in John ("Jack") Myles, an Irishman who led an adventurous life and was "well known in New Zealand and the South Seas in the last quarter of the nineteenth century" (76).

[3] Hayes and Pease (or Peese) are mentioned by name at the opening of Chapter 38 of *Lord Jim*. Gordan specifically cites Lubbock's study of the career of Hayes and Boldrewood's *A Modern Buccaneer*. Moser very briefly identifies the two (209), whereas Watts and Hampson (365-66) offer fuller information and provide dates. See Earnshaw, Lubbock, and Saunders for accounts of Hayes.

from anecdotes never recorded in print" (354), while Sherry focuses on a few particular details from Captain Sir Edward Belcher's *Narrative of the Voyage of H.M.S. "Samarang" during the Years 1843-46* (1848), suggesting that Brown's arrival at Patusan broadly resembles Belcher's at Gunung Tabor, that the name Brownrigg – the man Belcher had come to Berau to rescue – is echoed by "Brown," and that Brownrigg colluded with native factions in order to obtain his own ends, as Gentleman Brown does in relying upon Kassim (155-56) as a go-between. But neither real-life nor the "dull, wise books" (*CL2* 130) Conrad extensively relied upon appeared to offer sufficient material to build a large case.

Gordan was on the right track in considering the work of Rolf Boldrewood, a prolific English-born Australian writer of realistic tales of bush and squatter life, in fact one Thomas Alexander Browne (1826-1915), whose pen-name is borrowed from Sir Walter Scott's *Marmion*. Boldrewood's *A Modern Buccaneer* (1894) in which both the historical Hayes and Pease figure, is, however, mainly by Louis Becke, Boldrewood having bought a manuscript from him that he then reworked, with about two-thirds of the final book heavily indebted to it.[4] A summary of the book points to its thinly disguised autobiographical character: it "is the self-told story of Hilary Telfer who leaves his Sydney home for the sea at seventeen and becomes supercargo with the notorious Captain Bully Hayston, a gentlemanly scoundrel who trades in the South Seas" (Brissenden 1972, 22). In its general outlines, this is the story of (George) Louis Becke (1855-1913), an impressionist-realist Australian writer, significant in the development of a distinctly Australian literature.[5] If he is known at all in Conrad studies, it is because of a long letter of 22 August 1896 (*CL1* 302-04), in effect a review, Conrad wrote to T. Fisher Unwin about Becke's *A First Fleet Family*, a novel written in collaboration with Walter Jeffrey. This work, bearing the full title *A First Fleet Family: A Hitherto Unpublished Narrative of Certain Remarkable Adventures Compiled from the Papers of Sergeant William Dew of the Marines*, was published in Unwin's Colonial Library in May 1896 and sent to Conrad by Unwin (*CL1* 299). A boy's adventure tale, it follows the exploits of a English lad whose strong desire to go to sea sees him first involved in

---

[4] On Boldrewood and the history of *A Modern Buccaneer*, see Brissenden 1972, 22-24, and the *Dictionary of Australian Biography*.
[5] For a full discussion of Becke's writings, see Day.

South Coast smuggling and then joining the navy. He finally ends up in Australia, where he marries a squire's daughter and becomes a prosperous tenant farmer. Conrad objected strongly to the conventionality of the plotting and the lack of psychological verisimilitude. He confessed himself "furious with Mr. Becke" (*CL*1 303), and bewildered as to why Becke should have attempted such a book at all, given the interests and South Seas setting of his previous work. Aside from Conrad's having wasted part of his honeymoon in reading such a ploddingly crafted book at a moment when he was inching towards the writing of *The Nigger of the "Narcissus,"* both the length and tone of the outpouring seem disproportionate to Becke's offence. Conrad's true dissatisfaction lies with Becke's having abandoned the vein he excelled in in *By Reef and Palm* (1894) – the South Sea yarn – and for foregoing the technical skills that Conrad admired in that collection of short stories: "Strangely enough I have been, only the other day, *reading again* his *Reef and Palm.* Apart from the great interest of the stories what I admire most is his perfect unselfishness in the telling of them. The sacrifice of his individuality in the interest of the work. He stands magnificently aloof from the poignancy and humour of his stories. A thing I could never do – and I envy him" (*CL*1 298; emphasis added).

Becke, in fact, looms slightly larger in Conrad's early career than has been recognized. Early reviewers casually compared Conrad to Becke;[6] Conrad himself met him sometime in the later part of 1896;[7] and as a fellow writer in Unwin's stable – and a highly successful one at the outset of his professional writing life[8] – Becke's writing may have pointed out a direction that Conrad, at least very briefly, toyed with. Conrad clearly read Becke's early fiction with interest, perhaps in an attempt to gauge his own

---

[6] See, for example, reviews of *Almayer's Folly*, *The Nigger of the "Narcissus,"* and *Lord Jim* in the *Athenaeum, Illustrated London News,* and *Book Buyer*.

[7] In early August 1896 (*CL*1 298), Conrad missed meeting Becke, who was in London while Conrad was in France. If Conrad's "1895 or six" is reliable, then their meeting must have occurred after his return from Brittany in September 1896.

[8] Published in Unwin's Autonym Library in November 1894, *By Reef and Palm* went through two printings in the year of its publication, and a further two the year following. Most of the stories collected in the volume had originally appeared in the *Sydney Bulletin*. The rudimentary state of bibliographical research on Becke disallows establishing whether Conrad might have first become aware of them during his stints in Australia.

market appeal. His recollection of his single meeting with Becke was more dismissive than the actual circumstances seem to warrant: "I saw L. Becke once in 1895 or six in a publisher's office and I must say I wasn't favourably impressed then. I haven't read many of his books. Reef & Palm was the last I looked at I think" (to A. T. Saunders, 26 January 1917).[9] The unnamed publisher is, of course, Unwin, then publishing both fledgling writers. Some twenty years after his contact with Becke and his writings, Conrad understandably enough misremembered the exact title of Becke's book. Having read *A Fleet Family*, he had read at least one work later than *By Reef and Palm*. As his eloquent praise in his letter to Unwin establishes, he was favourably impressed with Becke's Flaubertian aloofness of method if not with the man who had actually had dealings with Bully Hayes.

Becke has fared little better at the hands of the few Conrad critics who mention him. Ian Watt, while noting Conrad's admiration for his work, states that there is "little reason to suppose that Conrad was particularly indebted" to him (1994, lii),[10] and while Andrea White draws passing attention to Becke in her extensive discussion of turn-of-the-century adventure writers, the link is not pursued (1993, 106). To employ her useful phrase, he does, however, make up part of "the shaping discourse" of Conrad's early fiction, and this essay will now pursue in what ways this may have occurred, emphasizing in particular how Becke's stories about Bully Hayes and Ben Pease served to contribute to the shaping of Gentleman Brown in *Lord Jim*.

Conrad's warm admiration for *By Reef and Palm* appears to have had only a minor echo in his work: he was possibly indebted to the volume's introduction by the Earl of Pembroke for drawing his attention to Alice Meynell's 1891 essay "Decivilized,"[11] to which he alludes in his "Author's

---

[9] Coincidentally, Saunders himself had a particular interest in Hayes, having authored two pamphlets on him; see Saunders.

[10] Watt's earlier formulation of his discussion in *Conrad in the Nineteenth Century* (43) did not specifically exclude Becke as a possible influence.

[11] In 1920, Conrad claimed that reading Meynell's essay had engendered his preface (*Almayer's Folly* 200); however, mention of the essay in the Introduction to *By Reef and Palm* is considerably closer in time to the writing of Conrad's "Author's Note" than to its original publication, and the Note's opening suggests second- rather than first-hand knowledge of it: "I am informed that in criticising that literature which preys on strange people and prowls in far off countries, under the shade of palms, in the

Note" to *Almayer's Folly*. The Earl of Pembroke, defending the subject matter of Becke's tales, offers the following observation:

> It is open to any one to say that these tales are barbarous, and what Mrs. Meynell, in a very clever and amusing essay, has called "decivilised." Certainly there is a wide gulf separating life on a Pacific island from the accumulated culture of centuries of civilisation in the midst of which such as Mrs. Meynell move and have their being. And if there can be nothing good in literature that does not spring from that culture, these stories must stand condemned. But such a view is surely too narrow. Much as I admire that lady's writings, I never can think of a world from which everything was eliminated that did not commend itself to the dainty taste of herself and her friends without a feeling of impatience and suffocation. It takes a huge variety of men and things to make a good world. And ranches and cañons, veldts, and prairies, tropical forests and coral islands, and all that goes to make up the wild life in the face of nature or, among primitive races, far and free from the artificial conditions of an elaborate civilisation, form an element in the world the loss of which would be bitterly felt by many a man who has never set foot outside his native land. (16-17)

Conrad's "Author's Note" echoes the basic point of Pembroke's preface, taking issue with the proposition that fiction has any limits of psychological or geographical range.

The fourteen short stories themselves, sometimes slightly lurid tales of fate and passion in the South Sea Islands, are strikingly written in what might be called proto-Conradese, with native dialect rendered in the rhythms and manner resembling that of Conrad's earlier Malay fiction: "And so thou hast left Samoa to come here to be devoured by this fat hog of a Dutchman! Dost thou know, O foolish, lovely one, that she who mates with a *Siamani* (German) grows old in quite a little time . . ." (31).[12] Local colour, comprising snatches of native languages, the odd untranslated word accessible through context, and the highly ornate locutions that stand in for native speech patterns, is a strong element throughout the stories. More

---

unsheltered glare of sun beaten beaches ... a lady – distinguished in the world of letters – summed up her aversion from it by saying that the tales it produced were 'decivilised'" (*ibid*., 3).

[12] No attempt is being made here to suggest that Becke influenced Conrad's dialogue, but the comparison is possibly not without interest for its linguistic representation of the Other.

important, perhaps, is the focus of the subject matter: solitary Englishmen, living alone of their kind on far-flung Pacific islands often in the thrall of beautiful native women. This plot element possibly accounts for the Introduction's distinguished pedigree and its attempt to naturalize the tales for the drawing-rooms of the morally proper. In any case, there are echoes of the basic plot element in *An Outcast of the Islands* and *Lord Jim*, novels in which "native wives" play significant roles.

Pace Gordan, there are in the latter novel at least vague echoes in the Gentleman Brown segment from Boldrewood's *A Modern Buccaneer*, a major contemporary source for the careers of the two American desperadoes mentioned in *Lord Jim*, for if indeed they were "notorious South Sea adventurers and pirates," as Moser describes them (1996, 209n.), their fame was broadcast to the wider world by Becke, through Boldrewood, as well as through the two volumes of stories published under Becke's own name. Becke's knowledge of Hayes, called Hayston in *A Modern Buccaneer*, came at first hand: he had dealings with him in the Marshall Islands and eventually quarrelled with and became estranged from him (Pembroke, 13-14). The chapter "The Brig *Leonora*" in *A Modern Buccaneer* contains an episode that vaguely resembles Brown's arrival at Patusan, where, after having made his way from the coast, he finds, to his disappointment, Jim already firmly ensconced. In *A Modern Buccaneer*, Hayston desires to dislodge a trader, a bloodthirsty ruffian whom he himself established on Drummond Island in the Gilbert Group, and who has double-crossed him in his dealings. Leaving his brig in the hands of a "Fiji half-caste" (54), Hayston makes his way to the town of Utiroa in a longboat, arriving to find a large crowd of armed and hostile natives. After he placates their hostility, the awaited confrontation between him and Jim, his errant trader, gets under way. Hayston goes to it deliberately unarmed, quickly bests Jim in physical combat, and takes him into custody, replacing him with another man and promising to put him ashore elsewhere. Whether Conrad made any use of this material is, of course, a matter of speculation. If he did so at all, it was mainly to stimulate his own inventiveness. The trader Jim, "an unscrupulous and remorseless ruffian" with a "heavy red moustache and bloodshot eyes" (58), bears little resemblance to Conrad's villain Brown, who is cut in an altogether more sinister mould, but Hayston himself does in his overweening self-confidence and braggadocio. Perhaps stronger is the echoing of the story's situation: the position of the entrenched trader upriver, the confiding of the brig to the Fijian,[13] the journey from the coast to the town in a longboat, the large and hostile reception that greets Hayston on his arrival, and the delayed confrontation between the two men. Little more can be made of this, and rather than an example of direct influence, the helpful term "shaping discourse" seems more appropriate to the intertextual relationship.

Although the Earl of Pembroke's Introduction makes something of both Hayes and Pease, the latter described as "a degenerate sort of pirate who made his living by half bullying, half swindling lonely white men on small islands out of their cocoanut oil, and unarmed merchantmen out of their stores" (10), Bully Hayes is only passingly mentioned in *By Reef and Palm* in the story "The Fate of the *Alida*." He makes a brief appearance in "The Cook of the *Spreetoo Santoo*" and is alluded to in "Lupton's Guest: A Memory of the Eastern Pacific" in Becke's *The Ebbing of the Tide: South Seas Stories*, a collection of twenty-one yarns published by Unwin in 1896 in the wake of the success of Becke's previous volume. The latter story significantly fleshes out the character of Ben Peese,[14] "the handsome, savagely humorous, and voluble colleague of Captain 'Bully' Hayes, the modern rover of the South Seas" (360), and is possibly the direct source for Conrad's epithet "mellifluous" (352). The story describes Peese as having a "pleasant voice that had in it always a ripple of laughter – the voice and laugh that concealed his tigerish heart and savage vindictiveness" (361). The dialogue given to Peese extends the narrative description of his voice and justifies the adjective "voluble." His greeting of Lupton, an English trader living on an island in the Paumotu Group, is in a class dialect and has a "mellifluous" character, to evoke Conrad's word, that establish a dissonance between his occupation as a pirate and brigand and his mastery of *les convenances*: "'How are you, Lupton, my dear fellow?' said Peese, as the trader gained the deck, wringing his hand effusively, as if he were a long-lost brother. 'By Heavens! I'm glad to meet a countryman again, and that countryman Frank Lupton. Don't like letting your hand go'" (362).

Two other aspects of Peese's character and story are of interest as possible "shaping discourses" for Gentleman Brown. First, Becke presents

---

[13] In *Lord Jim*, "a Chinaman and a lame ex-beachcomber of Levuka" (367) are left in charge. Levuka is a Fijian port town, but the text suggests that the character in question is not a native and merely an expatriate drifter of the kind frequent in Becke's fictions.
[14] Becke's story uses this spelling, whereas Conrad follows the spelling of the Earl of Pembroke's Introduction.

Peese in the guise of an English gentleman in speech and manner, in contrast to the American origins of the historical Pease. Secondly, the story specifically recalls Peese's stealing of a ship in the Philippines: "Peese ... from former associations, had a way of drifting into the Spanish tongue – and prisons and fetters – which latter he once wore for many a weary day on the cruiser *Hernandez Pizarro* on his way to the gloomy prison of Manilla [sic]" (365). The episode is also recalled in *A Modern Buccaneer*: "A daring act of piracy – seizing a Spanish revenue vessel under the very guns of a fort – and working her out to sea with sweeps, outlawed him. Caught at one of his old haunts in the Pelew Islands, he was heavily ironed and put on board the cruiser *Hernandez Pizarro*, for conveyance to Manila, to await trial" (73). The prison motif is a vivid aspect of Gentleman Brown's psychology, but may obviously be an invention without a specific source behind it; but Brown's theft of a Spanish vessel and connection with the Philippines suggest that Conrad may have been mingling some elements of the story of the historical Pease with materials picked up elsewhere, in the manner that Gordan suggested. In *Lord Jim*, the episode is complex, with Brown, having been arrested and towed by a Spanish patrol cutter, managing to bribe a government official and to steal "a good stout coasting schooner lying at anchor in the little bay" (354). It would be pushing the slight evidence too far to assert outright that Gentleman Brown is based on Becke's recollections and fictionalizing of Ben Pease, but it is not to overstate that case that there is some likelihood that he contributed to him and to the atmosphere of the chapters in which he appears. Conrad's interest in Becke's work is established by his own account, and in light of his admiration for *By Reef and Sail* it seems likely that he read more of Becke than it and *A Fleet Family*.

That he read *The Ebbing of the Tide*, and, specifically recalled the story "Lupton's Guest" is further suggested by yet another character, Becke's criminal "Mr. Brown," and to similarities to the final phase of Gentleman Brown's life. Peese arrives off Lupton's island to land a passenger, who has paid him for the favour:

> The passenger's appearance, so Lupton told me, "was enough to make a man's blood curdle," so ghastly pale and emaciated was he. He rose as Lupton entered and extended his hand.
> "My friend here," said the worthy little Ishmael, bowing and caressing his long silky beard, "is, ah, hum, Mr. Brown. He is, as you

will observe, my dear Lupton, in a somewhat weak state of health, and is in search of some retired spot where he may recuperate sufficiently —"
"Don't lie unnecessarily, sir."
Peese bowed affably and smiled, and the stranger addressed Lupton.
"My name is not Brown — 'tis of no consequence what it is; but I am, indeed, as you see in a bad way, with but a few months at most to live. Captain Peese, at my request, put into this lagoon. He has told me that the place is seldom visited by ships, and that the people do not care about strangers. Yet, have you, Mr. Lupton, any objections to my coming ashore here, and living out the rest of my life? I have trade goods sufficient for all requirements, and will in no way interfere with or become a charge upon you." (363-64)

Mr. Brown's anonymity, his grotesquely emaciated condition, and status as an outsider, like Lupton himself, are suggestive of Conrad's Brown in his final days in Bangkok, while the courtly behaviour and drawing-room dialogue, signally at odds with the locale and transaction, establish a "gentlemanly" context. After this point, Becke's story moves off wholly into the South Sea yarn, with "Mr. Brown's" identity and criminal past only finally revealed to Lupton after Brown's death: having killed his wife and her lover, he was imprisoned in St. Quentin but managed to escape from America to the remotest of islands in the South Seas. Acting the good Samaritan, Lupton has unknowingly played host to a murderer. The story plays up the shock-value of this delayed information, but leaves the themes of deception, self-deception, the nature of justice and social obligation undeveloped.

Although Conrad may have found ready-to-hand elements of character and psychology in Becke's South Sea yarns, their more important influence possibly lies in their basic settings: Englishmen living with native "wives" in remote corners of the South Pacific among easy-going societies that were the prey of brigands and pirates from the "outside" world. Becke's stories, moreover, suggest thematic concerns that Conrad takes up more forcefully and with much more artistic impact. While piracy was a day-to-day reality both in the Malay and South Seas islands of the novel's period, its significant thematic role in *Lord Jim* is to reaffirm the fragility of organized society. Greed, lawlessness, and the atavistic "will to live" that Conrad's "pirate" Gentleman Brown embodies help bring out the character of Lord Jim. Although Cornelius has these traits, he is too contemptible a figure to serve as an effective oppositional or mirror figure and a character of Brown's stature in required for purposes of thematic contrast. The confrontation between the "gentleman" pirate and the "Lord" of Patusan, whatever its vividly dramatic function, primarily, then, serves to develop and strengthen the novel's thematic interests, and Conrad thus turns to good use the sea outlaws he encountered in Louis Becke's stories.

WORKS CITED

Becke, Louis. *By Reef and Palm* (1894) and *The Ebbing of the Tide* (1896). Reprint. London: T. Fisher Unwin, 1914.
Belcher, Capt. Sir Edward. *Narrative of the Voyage of H.M.S. Samarang during the Years 1843-46*. London: Reeve, Benham, and Reeve, 1848.
Boldrewood, Rolf. *A Modern Buccaneer*. London: Macmillan, 1894.
Brissenden, Alan. *Rolf Boldrewood*. Australian Writers and Their Work. Melbourne: Oxford University Press, 1972.
Browne, Lt. Cmdr. Andrew K. M. "An Original for 'Gentleman' Brown." *Conradiana* 26.1 (1994): 76-79.
Conrad, Joseph. Letter to A. T. Saunders, 26 Jan. 1917. Archives Dept., Public Library of South Australia, Adelaide.
Day, A. Grove. *Louis Becke*. New York: Twayne Publishers, 1966.
Earnshaw, John. "Hayes, William Henry (1829?-1877)." *Dictionary of Australian Biography: 1851-1890*. Melbourne: University of Melbourne Press, 1974.
Gordan, John Dozier. *Joseph Conrad: The Making of a Novelist*. Cambridge, MA: Harvard University Press, 1940.
Lubbock, Basil. *Bully Hayes: South Sea Pirate*. London: M. Hopkinson, 1931.
Meynell, Alice. "Decivilised." 1891. In *Almayer's Folly*, edited by Owen Knowles, 190-92. London: Dent-Everyman, 1995.
Moore, T. Inglis. "Browne, Thomas Alexander (1826-1915)." *Dictionary of Australian Biography: 1851-1890*. Melbourne: University of Melbourne Press, 1974.
Moser, Thomas C., ed. *Lord Jim: Authoritative Text, Backgrounds, Sources, Criticism*. Norton Critical Editions. 2nd edn. New York: Norton, 1996.
Pembroke, The Earl of. "Introduction." In *By Reef and Palm* by Louis Becke, 1894, 9-18. Reprint. London: T. Fisher Unwin, 1914.
Review of *Almayer's Folly*. *Athenaeum*, 25 May 1895: 671.

Review of *Lord Jim*. *Book Buyer* 22 (1901): 63.
Review of *The Nigger of the "Narcissus." Illustrated London News*, Jan. 1898: 50.
Saunders, A. T. *Bully Hayes, Barrator, Bigamist, Buccaneer, Blackbirder, and Pirate: An Authentic Life of William Henry Hayes of Ohio or New York, U. S. A; born 1829, killed 1877*. Perth: Sunday Times, 1915.
——. *Bully Hayes, Louis Becke and The Earl of Pembroke*. Adelaide: n.p., 1914[?].
Sherry, Norman. *Conrad's Eastern World*. Cambridge: Cambridge University Press, 1966.
Van Marle, Hans, and Pierre Lefranc. "Afloat and Ashore: New Perspectives on Topography and Geography in *Lord Jim*." *Conradiana* 20.2 (1988): 109-30.
Watt, Ian. *Conrad in the Nineteenth Century*. London: Chatto & Windus, 1980.
——. "Introduction." In *Almayer's Folly*, edited by Floyd Eugene Eddleman and David Leon Higdon, xxi-lxiv. Cambridge: Cambridge University Press, 1994.
Watts, Cedric, and Robert Hampson. Notes to *Lord Jim*, edited by Cedric Watts and Robert Hampson, 353-66. Harmondsworth: Penguin, 1986.
White, Andrea. *Joseph Conrad and the Adventure Tradition*. Cambridge: Cambridge University Press, 1993.

THE MISSING CREW OF THE *PATNA*

Gene M. Moore
Universiteit van Amsterdam

Joseph Conrad's respect for the work of ordinary seamen has long been recognized. Early writings like *The Nigger of the "Narcissus"* and "Youth" celebrate the solidarity of officers and crewmen engaged in a common struggle for survival, and the ordinary sailors who man the *Narcissus* and the *Judea* receive Conrad's full attention. Despite the instability of its narrative voice, *The Nigger of the "Narcissus"* comes increasingly into focus as a story told from the perspective of an anonymous crew member who speaks for his shipmates and ends by paying them a famous farewell tribute: "Haven't we, together and upon the immortal sea, wrung out a meaning from our sinful lives? Good-bye, brothers! You were a good crowd" (173). In "Youth," Marlow is second officer of the *Judea*, yet he lives in close and attentive proximity to the crewmen, who receive exemplary treatment from the ship's elderly master. When the *Judea* is tossed about in a gale, the hands are ordered out of the deck-house "to sleep in the cabin – the only safe place in the ship" (13); and when the ship must finally be abandoned, this is done in an orderly and even loving manner, beginning with the youngest ordinary seaman (33). Many passages in *The Mirror of the Sea* testify to Conrad's respect for ordinary sailors, and as late as 1918, in "Tradition," he paid eloquent tribute to the heroism of merchant seamen in the First World War. Why, then, is this regard for the crew and concern for its welfare absent from Conrad's account of the voyage of the *Patna* in *Lord Jim*?

One might reply that Conrad was fond only of white or European sailors, and not of native crews; yet there is ample evidence (in "The End of the Tether" and *The Rescue*, for example) of his respect for the eyesight and insight of native sailors who often see and understand more than their white masters. Or perhaps the answer lies in Conrad's tendency to idealize or identify with the crews of sailing vessels (like the *Narcissus* and the

Judea) while feeling relatively little sympathy for the crews of steamships (like the *Patna*). Unlike the crew of the *Patna*, many of the crew members of Gentleman Brown's sailing ship are introduced individually, and their disreputable captain thinks of them as individuals: "They were sixteen in all: two runaway blue-jackets, a lanky deserter from a Yankee man-of-war, a couple of simple, blond Scandinavians, a mulatto of sorts, one bland Chinaman who cooked – and the rest of the nondescript spawn of the South Seas" (356) – including one daring Solomon Islander who is described as "the best man of the whole gang" (355). In *Typhoon*, the crew of the steamer *Nan-Shan* is portrayed with what F. R. Leavis called a "heroic sublimity" (1948, 185). In any event, the virtual absence of all reference to the crew of the *Patna* remains a mystery whose solution can shed light on the characters of Jim and Marlow, on the sense of solidarity expressed in Marlow's phrase "one of us," and on the aristocratic bias of a "lord" who is "very smart aloft" (6), but perhaps seeks out the heights so as not to have to look upon the real world of work.

The crewmen of the *Patna* are so hard to spot that readers and critics have often discussed the novel as if the five Europeans and the "eight hundred pilgrims (more or less)" were the only people on board. But these "five whites" (14,16) – the total complement of officers and engineers – are hardly enough to do the job, even in such a loosely run and disreputable ship as the *Patna*. Steamships generally require smaller crews than sailing vessels, but it is obvious that with only "the captain, the mate, and two engineers" (82) plus George, the "donkey-man" who "[a]cted third engineer" (107), the *Patna*, a steamer of some 1400 tons (30), is seriously understaffed.[1] And if there are not enough officers, the crew is reduced to the point of invisibility. The first narrator tells us that "The five whites on board lived amidships, isolated from the human cargo" (16); but they appear to be even more isolated from the crew, whose existence is registered only by the noises they make deep in the bowels of the ship:

> Above the mass of sleepers a faint and patient sigh at times floated, the exhalation of a troubled dream; and short metallic clangs bursting out suddenly in the depths of the ship, the harsh scrape of a shovel, the violent slam of a furnace-door, exploded brutally, as if the men handling the mysterious things below had their breasts full of fierce anger: while

---

[1] If expressed in terms of the number of crewmen per tons of cargo, the crews of steamships were actually larger than those of sailing vessels; see Brassey, p. 25.

the slim high hull of the steamer went on evenly ahead, without a sway of her bare masts, cleaving continuously the great calm of the waters under the inaccessible serenity of the sky. (19)[2]

In the following paragraph, the smoke of the steamer's engines – the visible sign of the work being done down below by the "angry" stokers – is literally dissolved away in an atmosphere of quiet nocturnal reverie: "The only shadow on the sea was the shadow of the black smoke pouring heavily from the funnel its immense streamer, whose end was constantly dissolving in the air. Two Malays, silent and almost motionless, steered." The helmsmen are silent and still, as befits the mood of Jim's daydreams. Shortly before the collision occurs, the noise of ash-buckets again proclaims the existence of the crew in the form of a noisy disturbance (20).

The first mention of the crew in Marlow's narrative occurs in Chapter Six, after the first adjournment on day one of the official Inquiry, when Brierly complains that "This infernal publicity is too shocking: there he [Jim] sits while all these confounded natives, serangs, lascars, quartermasters, are giving evidence that's enough to burn a man to ashes with shame" (67). The *Patna* is "owned by a Chinaman" and "chartered by an Arab" (14), but is presumably registered in Singapore and thus flies the Red Ensign; and Brierly is appalled that her shameful abandonment should expose the dignity of the merchant marine to general laughter and derision (as Marlow puts it) "from whites, from natives, from half-castes, from the very boatmen squatting half-naked on the stone steps" (36). With the exception of the two Malay helmsmen whose testimony is heard on the following day, Brierly's comment is the only indication that crew members were summoned to give testimony, and his suggestion that they testify volubly and in large numbers stands in sharp contrast to their passivity during the actual abandonment, in which they evidently played no role at

---

[2] Jameson takes this sentence as a key example of what he calls Conrad's "aestheticizing strategy," a typically modernist sidestep in which the "real" world of labour and material production appears only in the guise of impressionistic images (215, 230). Jameson's remark certainly applies to Jim, for whom the work ethic can only be a "work aesthetic" that finds expression in his daydreams. The very structure of Conrad's sentence, beginning with a "dream" and ending in "inaccessible serenity," frames and dissolves the angry violence of the stokers in a vividly rhythmic cadence that culminates in a shower of soothing sibilants. As a cadet on a training-ship, Jim takes a similarly lofty view of the roofs and factory-chimneys on the horizon (6).

all. They certainly play no part in the interrupted account that Jim gives Marlow the following evening at the Malabar House. In fact, Jim mentions the crew members only once, here again as an immobile and silent element of the background, indistinguishable in sleep from the "mass" of sleeping pilgrims: "Some of the crew were sleeping on the number one hatch ... they kept Kalashee watch in that ship, all hands sleeping through the night, and only the reliefs of quartermasters and look-out men being called. He was tempted to grip and shake the shoulder of the nearest lascar, but he didn't"; and Marlow justifies Jim's failure to alert the crew on the grounds that he feared a noisy and tumultuous emergency involving "the stupid brutality of crowds" (87-88). The result is that the drama of the *Patna*'s abandonment is limited to the five Europeans, and witnessed only by the two silent Malay helmsmen who "meanwhile remained holding to the wheel" (97). Kalashee watch is casual watch, which might well at times have meant no watch at all, since it was apparently kept by "them" without supervision rather than by "us," despite the fact that in principle at least three crew members must be awake in a ship at all times: one at the helm, one as lookout, and one officer of the watch in command. The officers apparently kept a regular schedule, since we know that Jim was just about to go off his own watch when the collision occurs (20); but no mention is ever made of the quartermaster or the look-out at the time of the abandonment, and in their desperation to abandon the ship, the whites never think to wake any crew members to help them lower or man the boats. Jim says only that "The ship began to buzz fore and aft like a disturbed hive" (109), presenting the passengers and crew in terms of a metaphor from the collective world of insects.

Jim's concern for the fate of the eight hundred pilgrims sets him apart from his fellow officers, who think of their "human cargo" (16) only as "cattle" (15) or "vermin" (25). As Jim tells Marlow, his only distinct thought was of "eight hundred people and seven boats," and this phrase echoes obsessively, three times on a single page (87; the figure "eight hundred" is cited altogether some six times in the context of the inquiry; 110, 113). It should be noted that this figure corresponds with the number of passengers in the *Patna* – some "eight hundred pilgrims (more or less)" (14) – and thus evidently fails to include the crew, to whom Jim gives not the slightest thought beyond the sleeping lascar. For all narrative intents and purposes, the *Patna* is described as if it were effectively without a crew.

The significance of the *Patna*'s absent crew can be demonstrated by comparison with their presence in the story of the *Jeddah*, the historical pilgrim ship whose abandonment in 1880 has been recognized since 1923 as a primary source for the story of the *Patna*.³ At some 993 tons register, the *Jeddah* was only two-thirds the size of the *Patna*, but she was even more crowded with passengers. She also carried a substantial crew, and her officers and men (and women) played an active and complex role in the events that made her notorious. According to the Report of the Court of Inquiry held at Aden on the abandonment of the *Jeddah*, she had "a total complement of 953 as adult passengers" and "Her crew consisted of 50 souls all told, which number included the master, first and second mates, and third engineer, who were Europeans, and with the captain's wife, the only Europeans on board" (cited in Sherry 1966, 299).⁴ There were thus just over a thousand people aboard the *Jeddah*: 953 adult passengers plus 50 officers and crew. Like the *Patna*, the *Jeddah* had five European officers on board, but they were distributed differently: the captain, two mates, and the first and third engineers; plus a sixth European who was not an officer but the captain's wife – a difference that would have important consequences once the *Jeddah* became disabled.

The Report of the Court of Inquiry describes in detail how under near hurricane conditions, with high breaking seas, the boilers of the *Jeddah* worked loose from their fastenings. The ship took on water, and "All hands and passengers were then working at the pumps and baling" (299). Unlike the passive mass of pilgrims of the *Patna*, the passengers and crew of the *Jeddah*, now so near the end of their journey, were prepared to work hard for their survival. Despite these efforts, "In consequence of the

---

3 The *Jeddah* was first mentioned in connection with *Lord Jim* by Frank Swettenham in a letter to the *TLS* replying to Richard Curle's in the previous issue. Conrad's correspondence suggests that he read Curle's article both in draft and in print; and in view of later critical argument about whether Patusan should be imagined in Borneo or Sumatra, it is curious to note that Curle – with Conrad's approval, or at least without his objection – located the village "on the south coast of north-west Sumatra," and this location was also quoted incidentally in Swettenham's reply. Of course Patusan is not on the coast, but upriver "about forty miles from the sea" (220).

4 The list of Europeans given in the Inquiry's Report fails to mention the chief engineer, Baldwin, whose own version of the events appeared in the *Straits Times Overland Journal* (2 October 1880) and is reprinted by Sherry (310-11). Captain Clark's written statement published in the same newspaper (8 September 1880; Sherry, 309) lists "a crew of 50 men, 5 European officers and 953 adult pilgrims bound to Jeddah."

quantity of water in the stoke-hole ... every connection pipe was carried away, and the engine-rooms became untenable and a wreck" (299). Although there are chronological and other discrepancies in the Inquiry's report, it appears that the passengers and crew were busy pumping and bailing for at least twenty-four hours – and possibly for as long as four days and nights[5] – until around midnight on 7 August 1880, when "apparently some diminution took place" and the captain "ordered the boats to be got ready, provisioned, armed, and swung out" (300). This phrase is contradicted slightly by the following reference not to "boats" plural but to "a boat or boats": "Certain of the crew were then ordered shortly after to man a boat or boats; the bulk of the crew appear to have manned the boats."

At this point the drama of abandonment begins, and the language of the Inquiry's report becomes even more cautious and circumspect: "At this time the passengers appear to have become partially disorganized, and to have entertained the idea that the boats were going to leave the ship. The master then appears to have decided to hang the starboard lifeboat astern, and to remain in it with his wife and the first engineer and a boat's crew until daylight, being, he states, afraid of his own and his wife's life being attempted if he remained on board."[6] The equivalent of Jim's "jump" is described as follows:

> The starboard lifeboat was then about to be lowered, and the captain and his wife and chief engineer got into it. The captain's wife had to pass some 50 feet from the cabin to the boat. When the boat was lowered, the pilgrims commenced to throw boxes, pots and pans, and anything they could lay hands on, into the boat, and pulled the first officer, who was lowering the boat, off the rails; and seeing that they could not prevent

---

[5] In a letter to Syed Mahomed bin Alsagoff, the Managing Director of the Singapore Steam Ship Company, dated 20 August 1880, and published in the *Straits Times Overland Journal* on 13 September 1880, Cowasjee Dinshaw & Bros., Alsagoff's agents in Aden, reported that "the passengers ... tired after pumping 4 days and nights, and when Captain Clark found that all people on board are tired, they thought the ship must be foundered" (see page 111 in this volume).

[6] Note that in this account, the passengers are all but blamed for giving the captain the idea of leaving the ship: they first "entertain the idea" that boats may be lowered, and only then does the captain decide to seek safety by doing so. This episode resembles Conrad's comical account, in "Youth," of Captain Beard's sudden "jump" to save his wife when the *Judea* is rammed by a steamer in the port of Hull (9).

the lowering of the boat, they attempted to swamp it. The third engineer had in the meantime got into the boat, and the first officer found himself in the water, and was taken into it, and the boat was then cut adrift ...
(300)

The pilgrims were also attempting to prevent the second officer, who by this time was apparently the only officer left on board, from leaving in a second boat. When those already in the boat refused to come back on board, the pilgrims cut the falls "and it fell into the sea bow first from the fore fall being cut first, and all in it appear to have perished."[7] The pilgrims also found the second engineer (the one non-European engineer) attempting to flee in a third boat, but they "threw all the men back from her into the ship, and would not allow them to leave."[8] In each of these episodes, the pilgrims, who found little to entertain them in the idea of their own abandonment, appear to have shown a consistent determination – however "partially disorganized" – to prevent the officers from leaving the ship. This perfectly reasonable aspect of their conduct might cause us to cast a cold eye on the way in which Captain Clark and his first mate insist that the mate did not jump from the ship but was, in his own words, "thrown overboard by the Hadjis after a severe wound was inflicted on my hand, and ... afterwards picked up out of the water by Captain Clark and taken into his boat" (Sherry 69) The report also noted that "two pistol shots were fired in the direction of the pilgrims from the boat by the first officer" – presumably with a pistol found in the boat, and with the hand that was not severely injured.[9]

In the Inquiry's report, the final count of fatalities and survivors fails to square with the initial estimate of passengers, officers, and crew, thrice given as "nearly 1,000 souls on board." The boarding officer from the

---

[7] The assessor's report stated that cutting the falls caused "one end of the boat to fall first, and it is supposed threw the crew out, who were drowned" and added that "Nothing was ever seen of this boat."

[8] The Inquiry's report published in the *Straits Times* describes these passengers as "Lojis" or "Logis."

[9] In his 1988 monograph entitled *Lord Jim*, Batchelor gives a seriously misleading summary of the *Jeddah* incident at odds with the evidence available from the official documents and from Sherry. Omitting all mention that passengers and crew had worked at the pumps for at least twenty-four hours, and in spite of the conclusions drawn by the Court of Inquiry and the Assessor, Batchelor claims that "The Moslem pilgrims refused to help pump and instead, realizing that the crew and the European officers had lost control, armed themselves in order to take possession of the lifeboats" (61).

Antenor reported finding some twenty remnants of the *Jeddah*'s crew of fifty: "Three sailors, one topman, one syrang, eleven firemen, and one clerk, one fireman working his passage ... together with the second engineer and supercargo, and 992 passengers – 778 men, 147 women, and children 67, not counting infants in arms, were on board."[10] This totals 1,012 souls, and does not include the infants, the eleven (or eighteen) who died when the second boat was cut loose, or the twenty-one who escaped in the captain's boat, which would bring the total to at least 1,044 (or 1,051). In Conrad's novel, when the French Lieutenant boards the abandoned *Patna*, he finds only a serang and an Arab effectively in charge of the ship (137).

Lifeboats also figure differently in the cases of the *Jeddah* and the *Patna*. The abandonment of the *Jeddah* apparently involved three of the ship's boats, two of which were "lost" – the one in which the Captain fled, and the second boat which vanished after the falls were cut, drowning eleven people. The Court of Inquiry did not make an issue of the shortage of boats, commenting only that "it is not out of place to remark, that in their estimation nearly 1,000 souls on board a vessel of the tonnage of the 'Jeddah' was a greater number than should be allowed by any regulation, especially for a long sea voyage, as taken by the 'Jeddah,' and at a season when bad weather might naturally have been expected" (Sherry 305). In other words, the Court described the overcrowding of the *Jeddah* not in terms of the shortage of boats, but in terms of the ratio of passengers to tonnage, probably because there was as yet no regulation to require lifeboats for all passengers (nor would there be until after the *Titanic* disaster thirty-four years later). According to a letter published in the *Straits Times Overland Journal*, the *Jeddah* had a total of six boats, and "a fourth of the people on board would have loaded every boat to the gunwale" (cited in Sherry 53-54). By this count, each boat could hold a maximum of some forty people. The number of people who left the ship in the Captain's boat varies, but ranges from fifteen to twenty, indicating that the ship was only half as full as it might have been. The *Patna* has seven boats, enough for a maximum of some 280 people, as Jim confirms by noting that there were "three times as many [people] as there were boats for" (84). What is striking is that only one of the *Patna*'s boats is involved

---

10 The salvage judgement listed twenty-one crew members found on board, and added that the second engineer "was ignorant of navigation."

in her abandonment, and Jim's lifeboat could have held at least thirty more people. Jim is struck by the way in which his fellow officers "talked as though they had left behind them nothing but an empty ship" (115) – one empty not only of passengers but also of her crew.

A brief survey of the documents concerning the *Jeddah* is enough to show that it would have been virtually impossible for any novelist to dramatize the original events in their full complexity, and Conrad no doubt found it convenient for the sake of narrative economy to limit the number of actors to five and to treat the pilgrims as a helpless and inert mass. But there may also be another reason why he gave the *Patna* an improbably small crew. Conrad's hospitalization in Singapore after an injury in the *Highland Forest* has long been seen as a major source for the episode of the "falling spar" that disables and strands Jim in an Eastern port (11). There the connection is generally thought to end; instead of returning directly home, Jim ships out in the 1400-ton *Patna* carrying pilgrims to Mecca, while Conrad signs on as first mate of the *Vidar*, a 304-ton trading steamer sailing in the opposite direction, up the east coast of Borneo.

Nevertheless, as Sherry has shown, the *Vidar* was linked with the *Jeddah* by the curious fact that Augustine Podmore Williams had served as first mate of both ships. Jim's certificate is cancelled along with that of his German captain, "Gustav So-and-so" (160); but the first mate of the *Jeddah* received only a reprimand from the Court, and – unlike Captain Clark, whose certificate was suspended for three years – there was no official stain on his reputation.[11] In the language of the Court of Inquiry, Williams "may be said to have more than aided and abetted the master in the abandonment of his vessel. The Court consider it very probable that, but for Mr Williams's officious behaviour and unseamanlike conduct, the master would (by the first mate's own showing) have probably done his duty by remaining on the ship." But the Court needed more than probabilities, and concluded that "Had there been any evidence, except the first mate's own statement, on this point, the Court would have felt constrained to have put him on his trial also, they cannot therefore refrain from remarking that they consider that in this instance he has shown himself unfitted for his position as first mate on a crowded pilgrim vessel" (Sherry

---

[11] Some members of the Legislative Council in Singapore felt that Captain Clark's sentence was too light, and discussed the possibility of further sanctions under their own jurisdiction (see the proceedings cited below, pp. 122-29 in this volume); but there was no question of putting the first mate on trial.

305).¹² Williams continued to work, and served as first mate in the *Vidar* on three trading voyages from May to October 1882, some two years after the abandonment of the *Jeddah* and five years before Conrad held the same position, from 22 August 1887 until 4 January 1888 (Sherry 29, 80-81). If Conrad was reminded of the *Jeddah* by having thus followed, so to speak, in Williams's footsteps, it is perhaps also worth noting that although the *Patna* is nearly five times larger than the *Vidar*, she has exactly the same complement of officers, consisting of the captain, only one mate, and three engineers.¹³ In merging the notorious episode of the *Jeddah* with his own memories of the hospital in Singapore and its aftermath, Conrad may well have continued to "borrow" from the sequence of events in his own life even at the cost of creating a nautically impossible situation for the officers and crew of the *Patna* – or at least one so irregular and improbable as to have been worthy of mention.

A comparable sleight of hand occurs in Conrad's account of the Court of Inquiry, where the multiple layers of narrative and the disruptions of chronology make it possible for him to tell the story of the second day of testimony three times over, in three quite different and even incompatible ways. In Chapter 4, the frame narrator shows us Jim in the witness box, trying to answer painful questions in a "very loud" voice while "from below many eyes were looking at him out of dark faces, out of white faces, out of red faces, out of faces attentive, spellbound, as if all these people sitting in orderly rows upon narrow benches had been enslaved by the fascination of his voice" (28). At the end of this scene, Jim's

---

12 The Assessor's Report concurred, concluding that "the first mate should not be permitted to go in the ship again" (309). Ignoring these judgements, Batchelor tries to give Williams credit for being in fact the kind of hero that Jim aspired to be: "The Captain had his wife on board and became so anxious for her safety that his judgement was impaired and the young first mate ... effectively took control. He ordered lifeboats to be lowered and helped Captain Clark and his wife to board one of them" (61). Batchelor's claim that "Williams – like Jim – was the last officer to leave the ship" (62) ignores the death of the second officer and the detention of the second engineer.

13 According to Allen, "The *Vidar* during Conrad's voyages carried, besides himself as chief mate and Captain Craig, a chief engineer, James Allen, a second engineer, John C. Niven, a Chinese engineer, a serang or boatswain, eleven Malays in the crew, and eighty-two Chinese for loading and unloading the cargo in the ports where the ship would call" (185). Conrad does not mention the Chinese in his account of this voyage in *A Personal Record* (78-95).

eyes meet those of Marlow (32). Marlow then takes up the narrative and describes his reluctance to get into "the inquiry thing, the yellow-dog thing" (34) that leads him to Jim at the end of this second day of testimony. Marlow then interrupts his narrative to tell the story of Brierly, concluding it some thirty pages later with Brierly's effort to enlist Marlow's aid in bribing Jim to disappear. Brierly's talk with Marlow must occur on the first day of the inquiry, since Marlow says that it was only on the "Next day" (69) that his eyes met Jim's. (There is no textual evidence of Marlow's presence in the Court on the first day, and he meets Brierly in the street.) On the evening of the second day, Marlow and Jim dine together at the Malabar House, and Marlow witnesses Jim's efforts to explain what happened on the *Patna*.

The third account of the second day of testimony centres on the testimony of the two Malay helmsmen whose behaviour impresses Marlow. As he puts it, "Not in the least wonder of these twenty minutes [of the abandonment], to my mind, is the behaviour of the two helmsmen. They were amongst the native batch of all sorts brought over from Aden to give evidence at the inquiry" (98). Brierly has already complained to Marlow of the embarrassment of the testimony of "all these confounded natives" (67) on the first day of the inquiry; but the two helmsmen are not called upon to testify until the second day.[14] Moreover, it appears that the helmsmen do not speak English – a circumstance that, were it not for the disruptions of chronological sequence, might lead one to wonder if Brierly's embarrassment takes into account the probability that most of the "confounded natives" cannot understand Jim's testimony, nor could he understand theirs without the aid of a translator (and the local members of the audience in the Bombay court might well have difficulty with English as well as Malay). The Court provides an interpreter for the helmsmen, and Marlow recalls that when the shy younger helmsman is asked to state "what he thought of it [the *Patna*'s abandonment] at the time," the interpreter, after a "short colloquy," reports: "He says he thought nothing."

The older helmsman, to the contrary, has a great deal to say, and Marlow renders his speech largely in free indirect discourse, with no

---

[14] The calling of so many native witnesses is overlooked by Lippe, who charges that the Court is unfair to Jim, since he "is required to stand before it in the double capacity of main witness and accused" (63).

mention of pauses or interruptions for the sake of translation. With "patient blinking eyes," the old helmsman

> explained that he had a knowledge of some evil thing befalling the ship, but there had been no order; he could not remember an order; why should he leave the helm? To some further questions he jerked back his spare shoulders, and declared it never came into his mind then that the white men were about to leave the ship through fear of death. He did not believe it now. There might have been secret reasons. He wagged his old chin knowingly. Aha! secret reasons. He was a man of great experience, and he wanted *that* white Tuan to know – he turned towards Brierly, who didn't raise his head – that he had acquired a knowledge of many things by serving white men on the sea for a great number of years ...
> (98)

Critics have been of two minds about this passage. The helmsmen have often been seen as foils for Jim, examples of unquestioning steadfastness (in the tradition of old Singleton in *The Nigger of the "Narcissus"* who "steered with care" [89]).[15] At the same time, the helmsman's blind faith in the wisdom and power of the white man is ludicrous, recalling old Father Gobila's conviction, in "An Outpost of Progress," that "the white stranger [the former head of the outpost] had pretended to die and got himself buried for some mysterious purpose of his own, into which it was useless to inquire" (*Tales of Unrest*, 96). What distinguishes the helmsman from Father Gobila is the courageous way in which he stands up to Brierly, invoking his own vast experience and reproaching the "white Tuan" for his failure to understand the situation. Brierly, of course, remains unmoved by anything a "confounded native" might have to say; he does not even deign to raise his head. At this point, perhaps provoked by Brierly's attitude, the helmsman launches into a bizarre and memorable tirade:

> – and, suddenly, with shaky excitement he poured upon our spellbound attention a lot of queer-sounding names, names of dead-and-gone skippers, names of forgotten country ships, names of familiar and distorted sound, as if the hand of dumb time had been at work on them for ages. They stopped him at last. A silence fell upon the court, – a silence

---

15 Tanner, for example, claims that the helmsman's "incoherent jabbering" nonetheless "represents that tradition of reliability, efficiency and trust which Jim has betrayed, the honour which he has lost" (31). For a brief survey of critical comments on the role of the helmsmen, see Verleun 199-200.

that remained unbroken for at least a minute, and passed gently into a deep murmur. (99)

The helmsman's tirade is evidently being delivered not in English but in Malay; he has not only outrun his translator but also exceeded Marlow's limited capacity to understand Malay, leaving Marlow unable to register anything more than the proper names of skippers and ships, moments of "familiar and distorted sound" in which even the very names are "queer-sounding."[16] Marlow goes on to say that "This episode was *the* sensation of the second day's proceedings – affecting all the audience, affecting everybody except Jim, who was sitting moodily at the end of the first bench, and never looked up at this extraordinary and damning witness that seemed possessed of some mysterious theory of defence" (99). Like Brierly, Jim keeps his head down during the helmsman's speech, and remains unaffected by it.

If however this episode was indeed sensational, "affecting everybody," as Marlow claims, then why does it receive not the slightest mention in either of the two previous accounts of this second day of testimony? The Malay helmsmen are absent from the first narrator's description of Jim's efforts to testify, and they fail to receive even the slightest mention from Marlow in connection with the "yellow-dog thing" that follows immediately upon this session, or in the course of the long dinner with Jim that very evening. In effect, Conrad's disruption of chronology enables him in this instance to have his cake and eat it twice, by giving three disparate accounts of one day's testimony, each with separate emphases and narrative and thematic purposes. It would be easy to take this disregard of native testimony as typical of the way in which Eastern voices are often "silenced" in Western literature: Dain Waris, his "European mind"(262) notwithstanding, is given not a single line of dialogue in the entire novel; and as Marlow later says of Jewel, "To discover that she had a voice at all was enough to strike awe into the heart" (315). On the other hand, the Malay trilogy contains many scenes in which indigenous characters like Babalatchi or Mrs. Almayer are fully capable of speaking for themselves. The villagers in *Lord Jim* are, by way of contrast,

---

16 Marlow's limited command of Malay is signalled by his inability to follow Jim's speech in Patusan (249), although he does manage on other occasions to have "a quiet chat" with old Sura (266) and an "interview" with Doramin (273). On the importance of "implicit translation" in Conrad's Malay novels, see Houston.

relatively silent. The obscuration of the crew and the silencing of the helmsmen help to define the ethnocentric limits of Marlow's and Jim's perceptions of their maritime and narrative responsibilities.

Later, when Jim assumes command, so to speak, of his own ship of state in Patusan, his treatment of the various elements of his "crew" of villagers shows a similar neglect of their individuality.[17] Marlow, citing Stein, says that before Jim's arrival in Patusan, "utter insecurity for life and property was the normal condition" (228). As master, Jim creates a new sense of security, but despite his ideas for Patusan's improvement, he does not challenge the indigenous social structure based fundamentally on slave labour.[18] On a ceremonial visit to Rajah Allang, Marlow describes how "A few youths in gay silks glared from the distance" while "the majority, slaves and humble dependants, were half naked, in ragged sarongs, dirty with ashes and mud-stains" (228-29). Jim's government makes little effort to improve these wretched conditions. Instead, he delegates responsibility in practical matters to his first mate, Tamb' Itam, a stranger from the north and former paddler for Rajah Allang, whose devotion to Jim is characteristically extreme:

> There was something excessive, almost fanatical, in his devotion to his "white lord." He was inseparable from Jim like a morose shadow. On state occasions he would tread on his master's heels, one hand on the haft of his kriss, keeping the common people at a distance by his truculent brooding glances. Jim had made him the headman of his establishment, and all Patusan respected and courted him as a person of much influence. (270)

Marlow finds various means of accommodating the morality of Jim's position as a white "straggler" (224) caught between the ideals of light literature and the reality of human suffering. For instance, Marlow tends to make light of the omnipresence of slaves. Doramin's wife, a figure of Dickensian energy, "was constantly in movement, scolding busily and ordering unceasingly a troop of young women with clear brown faces and big grave eyes, her daughters, her servants, her slave-girls. You know how

---

17 For a suggestive study of the role of "crowds" in the novel, see Kerr.
18 Slavery was banned by the Dutch government in 1863, but remote Patusan is situated somewhere between Dutch-controlled parts of Sumatra and Aceh, a sultanate at war with the Dutch since 1873.

it is in these households: it's generally impossible to tell the difference" (256). The line between servant and slave is blurred again when Abdulla's slaves transfer their allegiance to Jim, as if by right of conquest. Marlow describes "Jim's workmen" euphemistically as "liberated slaves" (314), even though their liberation consists only of the replacement of one master with another. He plans to house them separately: "What he called 'my own people' – the liberated captives of the Sherif – were to make a distinct quarter of Patusan, with their huts and little plots of ground under the walls of the stronghold" (340); but the best Jim can do is only to "liberate" them once again at the end, when even the dreaded Tamb' Itam is afraid "to go out amongst the people" (408). Like Captain Clark, Jim also has his "wife" on board, but he can hardly be said to show much concern for Jewel's safety. Instead of Captain Clark's misplaced solicitude, Jim tells Jewel that "There is no escape" (412); he must go down with the ship this time, leaving her alone and unforgiving.

In conclusion, the way in which the crew of the *Patna* and (by analogy) the common people of Patusan fail to capture the serious attention of both Jim and Marlow is symptomatic of the dreamlike and light-literary atmosphere that prevents European officers and gentlemen from fully appreciating the reality of non-white, ungentlemanly work. Marlow is unwilling or unable to entrust Jim's guilty secret to Jewel, and, like a less gullible Intended, she charges him with lying, making the accusation significantly "in the native dialect" (318). Jim's "Eastern bride" is ultimately not Jewel, but his own sense of lost honour. As Marlow says, "He goes away from a living woman to celebrate his pitiless wedding with a shadowy ideal of conduct" (416), ignoring once again the human "crew" that needs and depends on him, and confirming once again his incurably romantic disdain for immersion in the destructive element of labour and responsibility.

WORKS CITED

Allen, Jerry. *The Sea Years of Joseph Conrad*. London: Methuen, 1965.
Brassey, Thomas, M.P. *British Seamen*. London: Longmans, Green, and Co., 1877.
Batchelor, John. *Lord Jim*. Unwin Critical Library. London: Unwin Hyman, 1988.
Curle, Richard. "The History of Mr. Conrad's Books." *Times Literary Supplement*, 30 August 1923: 570.
Houston, Amy. "Implicit Translation in Joseph Conrad's Malay Trilogy." In *English Literature and the Other Languages*, edited by Ton Hoenselaars and Marius Buning, 109-22. DQR Studies in Literature No. 24. Amsterdam – Atlanta, GA: Rodopi, 1999.
Jameson, Fredric. *The Political Unconscious: Narrative as a Socially Symbolic Act*. London: Methuen, 1981.
Kerr, Douglas. "Crowds, Colonialism, and *Lord Jim*." *The Conradian* 18:2 (Autumn 1994): 49-64.
Leavis, F. R. *The Great Tradition: George Eliot, Henry James, Joseph Conrad*. London: Chatto & Windus, 1948.
Lippe, Hans. "Reconsidering the *Patna* Inquiry in *Lord Jim*." *The Conradian* 15:1 (June 1990): 59-69.
Sherry, Norman. "Conrad's Eastern World: A Study of Sources." Ph.D. dissertation, University of Singapore, 1963.
———. *Conrad's Eastern World*. Cambridge: Cambridge University Press, 1966.
Swettenham, Frank. Letter to the Editor. *Times Literary Supplement*, 6 September 1923: 588.
Tanner, Tony. *Conrad: Lord Jim*. Studies in English Literature No. 12. London: Edward Arnold, 1963.
Verleun, Jan. *Patna and Patusan Perspectives: A Study of the Minor Characters in Joseph Conrad's "Lord Jim."* Groningen: Bouma's Boekhuis, 1979.

JOHN DOS PASSOS
ON *LORD JIM*

Robert W. Trogdon
Kent State University

When Doubleday, Page & Company began reprinting Joseph Conrad's works in America in 1914, they introduced his books to a new generation of American readers, many of whom would go on to become writers themselves. Authors such as F. Scott Fitzgerald, William Faulkner, Ernest Hemingway, and Robert Penn Warren all acknowledged the importance Conrad's fiction had on their writing, and it is easy to see how works such as *The Great Gatsby* and *All the King's Men* were modelled on the example provided by *Lord Jim* and *Nostromo*. One writer who is usually not seen as being influenced by Conrad is John Dos Passos, best known for his novels *Three Soldiers* (1921), *Manhattan Transfer* (1925), and the *U. S. A.* trilogy (1930-36). But this view must be modified in light of Dos Passos's review of the 1914 Doubleday, Page reprint of *Lord Jim*.

Dos Passos's essay appeared in the July 1915 issue of the *Harvard Monthly*. At the time, he was a senior at Harvard and the *Monthly*'s editor. As Townsend Luddington, one of Dos Passos's biographers, notes, much of his time at Harvard was spent reading works not assigned for his classes and serving his literary apprenticeship with the *Monthly*: "The spring of 1915 he read more of the moderns ... He read much of Samuel Butler, Compton Mackenzie, Conrad, de Maupassant, Meredith, and Synge, among others" (1980, 64-65). The articles he wrote on these authors reflected "an enthusiasm for the new and unconventional: a new literary subject here, a new technique there" (Pizer 1988, 12).

Dos Passos's essay on *Lord Jim* shows him to be an unusually perceptive reader. Unlike many, he did not emphasize Conrad's role as a writer of adventures. Dos Passos instead drew attention to Conrad's skill at handling a plot that does not follow a strict chronological order and his adeptness at switching point of view. Of particular interest to Dos Passos is the way Conrad created characters, noting that they "emerge with vivid distinctness."

Conrad's influence on Dos Passos's fiction is not readily apparent. His work is not included in Gene M. Moore's useful survey of Conrad's impact on the writing of a wide variety of twentieth-century literary figures, including such major American writers as Fitzgerald and Hemingway. Conrad's focus on individual characters in his novels, on their plight and development, seems antithetical to Dos Passos's desire to present a panoramic view of society as a whole. But a closer examination of his narrative method shows what he learned from *Lord Jim*. His use of multiple points of view – the "Camera Eye" and "Newsreel" sections of the *U. S. A.* trilogy – owe something to the way Conrad used different narrators to tell the story of Jim. In the final analysis, both authors were interested in the same thing: how the individual functions in society. For Conrad, this meant focusing on the individual; for Dos Passos, it meant focusing on the society.

Although Dos Passos's essay on *Lord Jim* is known to scholars of his work (it was previously republished in Pizer's collection *John Dos Passos: The Major Nonfiction Prose*), it has gone unnoticed by students of Conrad. It is not listed in the standard bibliographies: neither Ehrsam nor Teets and Gerber list it, and it likewise goes unmentioned in Secor and Moddelmog's extensive compilation of work on Conrad and American writers. The below transcription of Dos Passos's essay on *Lord Jim* is as it originally appeared in the serial publication, not Pizer's reprinting. No silent emendations have been made to the text.

Conrad's *Lord Jim*
By J. R. Dos Passos, Jr.

A strangely subtle character study is *Lord Jim*. It is the story of a young man, physically clean, and healthy, and charming, almost a boy, in fact, who is by nature and breeding "one of us," a gentleman; but who, by some minute flaw, fails under strain and plays the coward. He is a mate of an old hulk of a steamer, the *Patna*, that carries East Indian pilgrims to Mecca. The boat runs into a derelict; so that her forward compartment becomes filled with water, leaving only an old rusty bulkhead, too rotten to repair, between the native passengers and drowning. The white officers and engine-room crew, who turn out to be abject creatures, prepare to slip away from the steamer unnoticed. Through pure excess of imagination, of power to visualize the horrors of the wreck he is sure is imminent, Jim's ability to act is paralyzed. At last, just as the captain's boat is pushing off, without knowing why or how, he jumps into it, and takes his place beside the cowards who are leaving the ship and passengers to their fate. As soon as he realizes what he has done he is horrified; but there is no going back. From that moment he and all the world think him a coward.

It is with the inquiry into the desertion of the *Patna* by her officers that the novel really begins. (By a miracle, the ship did not sink, but was towed into port by a French man-of-war.) The only one with the pluck to face it out is Jim; the others vanish. From there on the story is a minute study, from the point of view of Marlow, the strange character who relates it, of Jim's subsequent life. Not even Marlow, however, can really understand Jim. He is constantly perplexed. His age, his caustic analytic temperament – everything combines to prevent his being in full sympathy with the boy.

"But as to me," he says in one place, after one of his early conversations with Jim, "left alone with the solitary candle, I remained strangely unenlightened. I was no longer young enough to behold at every turn the magnificence that besets our magnificent footsteps in good or evil. I smiled to think that, after all, it was yet he, of us two, who had the light and I felt sad. A clean slate, did he say? As if the initial word of each our destiny were not graven in imperishable characters on the face of a rock."

Not until the end of the novel, if there, does Marlow profess to understand the man he is telling about. With marvellous skill, Conrad leaves it to the reader to do that. The story ends with Jim's heroic, romantic death, still misunderstood by his friends, by the woman he loves, and by himself.

About Conrad's remarkable narrative method, nothing adequate has been written. It is so startlingly unique and so daring that one is hardly likely to give it its full credit. Or is it that its very freshness blinds us to its faults? The novel, or most of it, is told from the point of view of Marlow's strange and complex personality. With great art the close is written from the rabidly hostile viewpoint of Brown, an almost grotesquely repulsive adventurer, pirate, and cutthroat.

Chronological order is nearly entirely abandoned. The opening pages place you exactly in the middle of the story. Then the plot goes far back for a swift incident, a hint of the great turning point in Jim's life, at last returning to the chronological start of the narrative. The scene skips next to where Marlow is telling the story of the inquiry – "After dinner, on a veranda draped in motionless foliage and crowned with flowers, in the deep dusk speckled by fiery cigar ends. The elongated bulk of each cane chair harbored a silent listener. Now and then a small red glow would move abruptly, and expanding, light up the fingers of a languid hand, part of a face in profound repose, or flash a crimson gleam into a pair of pensive eyes overshadowed by a fragment of an unruffled forehead; and with the very first word uttered, Marlow's body, extended at rest in the seat, would become very still, as though his spirit had winged its way back into the lapse of time and were speaking through his lips from the past." Famed[1] in this scene, it goes on, interwoven, complex, taking sudden leaps forward and back, constantly changing the point of view. But out of what would seem to be utter confusion, incidents and characters emerge with vivid distinctness, but of a haze of conjecture, of personal opinions, of interplay of personality, the characters appear gradually, becoming sharper, more actual, with each change of focus. The result is amazing, almost incomprehensible. You are dazzled by the vividness of portrayal. Jim, Jewel, the pirates and the Malays, and even the whimsical and sardonic Marlow are immensely alive.

Behind them floats an atmosphere, a vast impression of romance made actual. Tropical jungles, sunbaked seaports, the glittering blue Indian Ocean, unite to give an impression of romantic strangeness, yet of truth. Even the hideous, gargoyle-like villains, Cornelius and Brown and the crew of the *Patna*, seem as real as the horrid leering faces you sometimes see at night in the streets under the sudden glare of an arc light. The setting and the strange minor figures form a marvellous background against which moves the story, seen through the prism of Marlow's personality.

Never could enough the [*sic*] written about Marlow, that remarkable figure behind which the author hides his own individuality. He is the teller of *Chance*, of *Youth*, and of many others in that series of novels that has carried delicate analysis and realism into the field of Herman Melville and Ballantyne. The mere fact that Marlow does not lose actuality and "roundness" in the process, that he does not become a bundle of phrases

---

[1] Possible misprint for "Framed."

and qualities, is one of the highest proofs of Conrad's uncanny power of characterization.

Indeed, Conrad's books are staggering achievements. You start with prejudices, with dislikes, you complain of his style; by the time you have finished you are cowed, wonderstruck. There is such a wealth of humanity in them; the treatment is so subtle! It is as though you were looking at life through some wonderful instrument, a microscope that, instead of magnifying, merely refines the outlines. Out of the mists and mis-apprehensions which cloud the minds of the characters, the reader has constructed for him actuality; but actuality refined upon, laid bare, as it were, made transparent.

The great joy of reading Conrad, apart from the romance of it, from the liveness of it, lies in the fact that his books act as a sort of mental grindstone. When you have finished such a novel as *Lord Jim* or *Chance*, your mind feels clearer, more efficient and capable than when you took it up. Your intellectual cobwebs have been blown away. You feel as if a little of Conrad's magic elixir had penetrated your own brain. But perhaps that is a priggish, ultra-literary pleasure to take in anything so full of color and humanity. In its romance, without a doubt, lies the fascination and the greatest enjoyment of Conrad's work.

WORKS CITED

Dos Passos, John. "Joseph Conrad's *Lord Jim*." *Harvard Monthly* 60 (July 1915): 151-54.

Ehrsam, Theodore G. *A Bibliography of Joseph Conrad*. Metuchen, NJ: Scarecrow Press, 1969.

Luddington, Townsend. *John Dos Passos: A Twentieth Century Odyssey*. New York: Dutton, 1980.

Moore, Gene M. "Conrad's Influence." In *The Cambridge Companion to Joseph Conrad*, edited by J. H. Stape, xx-xxx. Cambridge: Cambridge University Press, 1996.

Pizer, Donald. "Introduction." In *John Dos Passos: The Major Nonfiction Prose*, 12-16. Detroit: Wayne State University Press, 1988.

Secor, Robert and Debra Moddelmog, comp. *Joseph Conrad and American Writers: A Bibliographical Study of Affinities, Influences, and Relations*. Westport, CT: Greenwood Press, 1985.

Teets, Bruce E. and Helmut E. Gerber, comp. *Joseph Conrad: An Annotated Bibliography of Writings about Him*. DeKalb: Northern Illinois University Press, 1971.

NEWSPAPER ACCOUNTS OF THE *JEDDAH* AFFAIR

Gene M. Moore, compiler
Universiteit van Amsterdam

The link between Conrad's *Patna* and the real life *Jeddah* was first noted in Frank Swettenham's reply to Richard Curle's survey of "The History of Mr. Conrad's Books" published in *The Times Literary Supplement* for 30 August 1923. News of the sinking of the pilgrim ship *Jeddah* off Cape Guardafui on the night of 7-8 August 1880 was first spread by telegram from Aden, followed the next day by a second telegram announcing the ship's rescue with nearly one thousand passengers who had been abandoned by their European officers. Printed in newspapers, the telegrams gave rise to further letters and commentaries. Norman Sherry's Ph.D. thesis included as an appendix a number of photographs of pages from the Singapore weekly *Straits Times Overland Journal* containing material relevant to the *Jeddah* incident. When he revised and published his thesis as *Conrad's Eastern World*, Sherry transcribed four of the most important items, including them as Appendix C (pp. 299-309), namely: the Report of the Court of Inquiry in Aden, the Assessor's Report, and letters to the *Straits Times Overland Journal* from Captain Clark and Chief Engineer Baldwin. There is no need to reprint these here. Rather, a selection of items that have not been previously published, or published only in part, is offered below.

These additional materials reveal a wide range of public reaction to the news of the *Jeddah*, from Captain Carter's remark that the captain might well have been safer on the open sea than at the mercy of "wretched fanatics," to the vivid expression of Mr. Campbell's shame and indignation before the Singapore Legislative Council: "I think and I question whether any of us in the same situation would not have shot Captain Lucas Clark like a dog for his dastardly attempt to desert his vessel in such dire distress."

The items below are reprinted in chronological order. The punctuation and style of the originals have been reproduced, but obvious misprints have been silently corrected. The first three items are from *The*

Times of London, and consist of a letter from Captain Henry Carter describing his experiences in the pilgrim trade (14 August 1880), and two comments on Carter's letter. The remaining items, from the *Straits Times Overland Journal*, consist of: four commentaries that accompanied the publication of the report of the Court of Inquiry in the issue for 13 September 1880; the full text of the proceedings of the Legislative Council on 14 September, when the *Jeddah* case was discussed; and finally, the full text of the salvage judgement accorded in the Vice Admiralty Court of the Straits Settlements on 20 October 1881.

1. Captain Carter's Letter to *The Times*, 14 August 1880, p. 5.

THE ABANDONMENT OF THE *JEDDAH*

A Correspondent says that, pending the arrival of the details of the reported abandonment of the steamship *Jeddah*, with between 900 and 1,000 Moslem pilgrims on board, the following extract from a letter written to a friend in London by Captain Henry Carter, of *Obelisk* fame, shortly before his death on the 10th of January, last seems to suggest that the strange desertion of their ship by the captain and his chief officers may only too possibly have been prompted by a natural instinct urging them to trust themselves to the sea rather than face perils of a more dreadful kind. Captain Carter's last employment was in this pilgrim traffic, which, under date November 30th, 1879, on board the steamship *King Arthur*, then lying in the port of Jeddah, he thus graphically describes:

"No one who has not witnessed the pilgrims actually *en route* can form the slightest conception of the unromantic and unpicturesque appearance of these wretched fanatics. It is a pity that some philanthropist will not take the trouble to make the tour, and go on board one of the pilgrim vessels about to start on a voyage to Jeddah. There are horrors on board such a ship which no Christian has ever dreamt of, and none but those who grow rich by such wickedness can form any idea of what goes on in these vessels under the British flag – wickedness worse, by far, than was ever found on board a slaver. Only fancy 1,000 or 1,200 fanatics cooped up on the deck of a small vessel for 18 or 20 days, with no room to move, and little or no fresh air to breathe. There is no medical man to attend to their wants when sick, and but a limited stock of medicine on board. I lost seven pilgrims in about 10 days, and I firmly believe that prompt medical treatment by a doctor would have saved them all. Of course, if these wretched beings die *en route* to Mecca, their eternal happiness is assured, so that they generally seem glad to give up the ghost and fly to the realms of joy. I wish you could have seen some of our little scenes of excitement. You must understand that my 'batch' consisted of Turcomans, Arabo-Persians, and Bedouins. They all came on board armed to the teeth, but, of course, I had all their weapons taken charge of by my officers and locked up in safety. I mean all the weapons we saw. They take up their quarters in any part of the ship, and from the moment of embarkation set the captain and officers at defiance. One day I had occasion to give orders for the removal of some luggage, which I found placed on the steering-gear, and which, of course, interfered with the navigation of my vessel. I was informed by my officers that the owners of this luggage refused to shift it, and, on my insisting on obedience to my orders, I found about me 150 cut-throat Arabs, all armed and prepared to resist my authority. Discretion was the better part of valour, for my three officers and myself were the only Englishmen on board, so that the odds were too great, and I quietly gave way. I thus found I had not got possession of all the swords, daggers, and firearms, which grieved me much. We were often alarmed by cries of 'Fire!' but on only one occasion was it at all serious. In this instance some of these men had lighted a fire on the bare deck, in order to prepare some tea. Of course, a dry pine deck, with its oakum and pitch, was soon ablaze. Luckily it was the upper deck, so the fire was soon mastered. Had it happened below the result would have been terrible, for the 'tween decks would have filled with smoke, the confusion and panic would have rendered the pumps unworkable, the five boats would have been taken possession of and swamped, and a dense cloud of smoke would have been the quickly vanishing sign of a dreadful disaster. The ship and her living freight would have been among the 'missing.' A shocking scene occurred one very dark night, which convinces me of the savage nature of the men I had to deal with. It was reported to me at 10 p.m. that one of the pilgrims was dead. So I gave orders that the friends of the deceased should take the body to the lee side and prepare it for burial. This was being done, but in carrying the corpse across the deck the bearers happened to disturb some Persians who were asleep. Instantly there was a terrible uproar. Swords, daggers, and bludgeons were brandished; the corpse was nearly torn to pieces; and one of my officers who attempted to quell the disturbance, was thrown down. An implement, something between a tomahawk and a pickaxe, was aimed at his head, but a friendly hand was near, and his life was saved. I have carefully preserved this formidable weapon as a memento of such happy times. A few years ago a pilgrim vessel was stranded on one of the reefs in the Red Sea, and before any attempt could be made to get the ship off the captain and his officers were tied to the mast, and their throats were cut. When the wreck was discovered their bodies were found in this state, and out of the ship's 500 passengers 450 were drowned."

2. **To the Editor of *The Times* from "F. R. G." 17 August 1880, p. 8.**

Sir, – Having read in *The Times* of to-day the extract from Captain Carter's letter, I am in hopes that public attention will now be called to the frightful manner in which the pilgrim traffic is carried on and some steps be taken to put a stop to its flagrant evils.

My brother went out to Bombay as chief officer of the *King Arthur*, under Captain Carter's command, and at Bombay exchanged into a larger steamer engaged in the same trade. In his letters he has repeatedly described the state of affairs on board, and these descriptions quite bear out the facts as stated in Captain Carter's letter.

The following is an extract from a letter written at Calcutta last January:

"We arrived at Calcutta on the 2nd of January after a weary passage of 27 days. I told you in Aden we had smallpox on board; they took out ten people and put them in the hospital. After two days' delay we proceeded for Calcutta. On our way smallpox again broke out worse than ever. Then we ran short of coals and began to pull to pieces the woodwork of the ship in order to fire up, and, after great delay, succeeded in getting into Colombo. There they immediately put us into quarantine, but took out of the ship all the smallpox patients, 15 in number. We remained Christmas Day and the next day, so you may guess what a pleasant Christmas we spent, all diseases around us and hundreds of the pilgrims starving. They have to bring their food with them, but many of them are destitute. Forty-six of them died during the passage, some from disease and some from starvation. After we left Colombo smallpox again broke out, and as soon as we arrived in Calcutta we were again put in quarantine, but we were glad to get rid of the 1,200 filthy pilgrims. One baby was born, but it died before morning for want of attendance; we carry no medical man. The brutes will not help one another and we have nothing to do with them. However, as the mother was a deck passenger and was dying, we put her in an empty cabin, gave her good food, and pulled her through. Seven hundred of the pilgrims live between decks; the other 500 live on deck in the open air, rain or no rain."

The steamers engaged in the pilgrim trade are all, or nearly all, owned by native firms, although they sail under the British flag and carry British officers. These native owners make large profits out of the traffic, and the intervention of the law is the only chance of any attention being paid to the claims of humanity.

I am, Sir, yours faithfully,

F. R. G.

August 14.

3. To the Editor of *The Times* from "A Singapore Merchant," 17 August 1880, p. 8.

Sir, – It may interest your readers to know that no such horrors as those depicted by Captain Carter have been known in the pilgrim trade between Singapore and Jeddah, at any rate for many years past.

The trade is a large one, and is carried on in steamers, which have to comply with the regulations set forth in the Straits Settlements Passenger Acts, passed specifically to prevent over-crowding, &c.

The vessels have to undergo Government survey before loading, nor are they allowed to sail till the pilgrims on board have been counted by the harbour-master, to see that the number specified by the Act has not been exceeded, and that the necessary provisions for their comfort have been carried out.

The *Jeddah* is an iron steamer, was built specially for the trade at Dumbarton in 1872, is classed 100 A1 in Lloyd's Register, and has hitherto been the favourite ship with pilgrims.

I remain, Sir, your obedient servant,

A SINGAPORE MERCHANT

London, Aug. 16

4. The *Straits Times Overland Journal* of 13 September 1880 printed the report of the Court of Inquiry in Aden, prefaced with a series of related articles (pp. 1-4) including an editorial comment under the rubric "Summary of the Week," the text of a letter from the *Jeddah*'s agents in Aden to the owner in Singapore, a background report on various aspects of the pilgrim trade, and a survey of comments in the London papers.

[from "Summary of the Week":]

Public excitement has risen to fever heat here in surveying the conduct of Captain Clark, who is well known here, and his officers and Engineers in deserting the S.S. *Jeddah* in the open sea, and leaving over 1,000 helpless poor creatures, pilgrims, many of them women and children to a possible terrible fate. Words would fail any right minded man to express his indignation of the wretched cowardice displayed by this contemptible clique of would-be-sailors, who are a disgrace to their country, and a disgrace to their cloth. It is only to be hoped that the Bombay Government will not permit Captain Clark to escape from Justice, he is here now, realizing his property but unfortunately the Government of this Colony have no jurisdiction in the matter. His cowardice was exhibited in Indian waters, and its consequence, the loss of lives, is for the Indian authorities to decide upon and deal with. One result of the heartless behaviour of these Europeans will be that the Hadji trade generally will now be a subject for legislation. It is well-known that the poor Hadjis are often subjected to gross injustice, and it is a sin and a shame that the religious prejudices which dictate their pilgrimages to the tomb of their prophet are taken advantage of to impose penalties upon them which would never bear the calm investigation of an English Court of law. And in every ship connected with this trade the absence of a sufficient number of boats in case of wreck or disaster is prominently evident. Thanks to Mr. Campbell, to whom every credit is due for so speedily ventilating the matter, the conduct of the disgraced sailors who deserted their ship and then lied on arrival at Aden as to her foundering will form a subject for discussion at the next meeting of the Legislative Council. The finding of the Court of Inquiry held at Aden, which will be found in another column will, doubtless, be read everywhere with interest and its perusal will only convince every one that not a single redeeming feature can be found in the shameful behaviour of the miserable Europeans in whose charge were placed the lives of so many harmless and helpless poor people.

From *The Daily Times*, 8 September.

THE S.S. "JEDDAH."

MR. SYED MAHOMED BIN ALSAGOFF, Managing Director of the Singapore Steam Ship Company, has kindly placed at our disposal the following letter, which we print *verbatim et literatium*, from his Agents in Aden regarding the abandonment of the S.S. *Jeddah*, and which contains the only information he has received on the subject independent of Captain Clark's statement. The telegrams announcing the circumstance, which were received by Mr. Syed Mahomed, have been, it will be remembered, already published:

STEAMER POINT,
Aden, August 20, 1880.

SYED MAHOMED ALSAGOFF, Esq.
Managing Director,
Singapore S.S. Company,
Singapore.

DEAR SIR, – With deep regret we have to report you the sad circumstances of your good S.S. *Jeddah*.

Captain Clark came with Mr. Omar to our office at about 9 p.m. on the 18th inst., to our surprise, they reported that the S.S. *Jeddah* is foundered this side of the "Socotra" Island, and he himself and his wife, Syed Omar, 1st Mate, 1st Engineer and 21 others arrived per S.S. *Scindia*, and he, Captain Clark gave the Captain of the S.S. *Scindia* Rs. 700 as a remuneration for bringing them with food, &c., supplied to all people.

On the 11th instant at about 6 p.m. it was reported, and came into anchor about 7 p.m., the S.S. *Jeddah*, in tow of Messrs. Alfred Holt's S.S. *Antenor* which was more surprising when it was reported that she had foundered. Immediately on her arrival the authorities ordered the Police

Superintendent and Harbour Pilot to go on board, to see what was to be done, and of course our people as well as others went on board for anxiety of the ship and people reported [as] foundered; the water was only in the Engine room and nowhere else, the bearers of the Boilers broke down and Boilers shifted and whole cause in consequence of the Boilers on one side and the feed pumps gave way, and rapidly the water filled up the Engine room, with pumping of water day and night by passengers they tired after pumping 4 days and nights, and when Captain Clark found that all people on board are tired, they thought the ship must be foundered. The authority, on arrival of the ship, took charge to land passengers and to keep the ship in safe place, and for about 4 or 5 days they put their own men to pump water out of her and to get clean, &c. When your message came to us of course we guaranteed for expenses and to send the passengers to Jeddah and took charge of her and we have had a survey ourselves and Government had another survey on Engine room and Boilers, and the report we forward herein by which you will see what is wanted and we shall be able to do all work here. The second survey we called on the cargo, and glad to say it is not damaged. Copy of survey is herein enclosed. We shall have a Marine Survey on the ship and see what is deficient. At present we can see the sails are all broken in pieces and more lost, 2 life boats are lost, 2 compasses, 2 chronometers are gone, and we have to place whole of these before she is ready for sea. Capt. Clark has left his one chronometer on board.

The Court has finished the trial, and will give verdict this afternoon, and what we have heard is that Captain Clark will lose his certificate, but no one else be injured in any way.

The 2nd Mate is lost by jumping in boat when Captain Clark left the ship, and 3 Khallasees and passengers, in all 18 lives, are lost.

We telegraphed you to send a Captain and we believe you will find a good Captain in Singapore to engage him and send him by a first steamer; it will be much cheaper in long run than to engage here a stray one.

Regarding Officers and Engineers, we shall report you in our next.

Captain Clark has got leave to proceed on, and he is going to-day to Singapore with his wife per M. M. Co's steamer.

He has Rs. 710 to pay to Captain of the *Scindia* who brought them, which we have debited to the Company.

We shall send you copy of the Court decision on the trial in our next which will give full light on the subject, but it is a bad job done by Captain Clark.

About 300 passengers are already sent away at R. 10 each, and we shall send them as the opportunity may offer. The authorities do not like to keep them longer, fearing of sickness breaking out amongst them and may cause an epidemic in the place.

You may rest assured that we shall not fail to do all for the interest of the Company in a most economical way. We have received the credit for 810,000 and will draw as we may require. In meantime we close this in haste as the time of mail is quite near for closing at the Post Office.

We remain, Dear Sir,
Yours faithfully,
COWASJEE DINSHAW & BROS.

From *The Daily Times*, 10 September.

THE S.S. "JEDDAH."

THE fame of Captain Clark, who, we believe, is realising his property here with the object of leaving for England, has preceded him. The London newspapers publish the details, eagerly, of his desertion of his ship. For our own part we await the receipt of the evidence given at the court of inquiry at Aden, in a spirit of fair play, before we make any comments or draw conclusions. Most persons here have formed their opinions as to Captain Clark's conduct but until the whole of the facts are before us, we prefer to keep silent. The London *Standard* contains the following telegrams and general remarks on the subject. Mr. Syed Mahomed hopes to obtain the copy of the evidence given before the Court of Inquiry by the next mail, he has not received any letter from Aden by this mail:

Aden, 10 August. – The steamer *Jeddah*, of Singapore, bound for Jeddah, with 953 pilgrims on board, foundered off Cape Guardafui, on the 8th inst. All on board perished excepting the captain, his wife, the chief officer, the chief engineer, the assistant engineer, and 16 natives.

The survivors were picked up by the steamer *Scindia* and landed here.

Aden, 11 August, 7.50 p.m. – The *Jeddah*, which was abandoned at sea with nine hundred and fifty-three pilgrims on board, did not founder as reported by the master. She has just arrived here, all safe, in tow of the steamer *Antenor*.

Although the first telegram from Aden turns out, happily, to be unfounded, public attention will, no doubt, be attracted to what is known as the Pilgrim Trade. The tendency of the members of most religious persuasions to attach peculiar interest to certain spots supposed to possess especial sanctity is well known. Among none is this sentiment more strongly developed than with those professing the Mahomedan faith. With a very pious Mussulman, to visit the holy places at Mecca and Medina is the dream of a lifetime. From his earliest youth it is the one object of his ambition, and to gratify it he will put by, year after year, every piastre that he may be able to scrape together, and not absolutely required for the wants of himself and family. Nor is this surprising. He is taught by his religion that by visiting the places sacred to the memory of the Great Prophet he will expiate his past sins – and those who know him will admit that these are neither few in number nor limited in character – and will also do much to secure his eventual entry into Paradise. One of the most popular songs with which the Egyptian Mahometan regales himself has for its chorus the words, "Oh that I were at Mecca, that I might listen to the voice of the pigeons as they soar round the tomb of the Prophet." And in the greater number of Arab stories and romances the same idea manifests itself. Not only are the spiritual prospects of the true believer improved by a pilgrimage, but he also gains in the opinion of his fellow-men. His departure is witnessed by all his neighbours and acquaintances, who assemble to wish him farewell. It is, however, for his return that the greatest triumph is reserved. Weeks before the arrival of the caravan is expected his friends commence their preparations. His house is visited, and the outside ornamented with grotesque paintings in many colours. Varied as may be the details, the object is the same – namely, to show the triumph of good over evil. Huge lions and demons of various kinds are depicted chained to the earth, and rendered powerless by the influence of some good genius. The interior of his habitation is swept and garnished, and such members of his family as do not accompany him deck themselves for his return in their gayest clothes. When his arrival draws nigh he is met by a numerous [*sic*] cavalcade, the women on camels and donkeys, and the men on foot. Accompanied by them, and preceded by a band of musicians, the returning pilgrim, mounted on a white horse, is conducted to his house amid the applause of the spectators. People rush from among the crowd to catch a glimpse of his features, and struggle for the privilege of kissing his hand. Nor does his glory end with his life. A peculiar mark is placed over his tomb to mark the resting-place of the pious pilgrim, and his co-religionists at certain stated seasons pay solemn visits to his grave. Such being the celestial and terrestrial benefits derived from a pilgrimage, the Mahometan, in order to obtain them, cheerfully submits to every hardship and privation. The number of pilgrims increases every year, and, as may be supposed, people have not been slow to appreciate the advantage of supplying them with the necessary means of locomotion.

By far the greater number of pilgrims arrive by sea. Algeria, Morocco, Egypt, and the far East annually send pilgrims who are numbered not by tens but by hundreds and thousands. The favourite port of debarkation is Jeddah, and a scene of excitement such as few places present is witnessed there during the pilgrim season. Though of course interesting to the true believer at all times, it is principally at the Feast of Courban Bairam that the holy places are most attractive. It is then that the ceremony of killing a lamb in commemoration of the offering by Abraham of his son Isaac takes place, and to be present on this occasion is what most pilgrims try to arrange for. The ships in which the pilgrims are conveyed belong to all nationalities. Those which come from the adjacent ports in the Red Sea generally fly the Ottoman flag, but of those which arrive from more distant places by far the greater number carry the English ensign. The conveyance of these devotees has been found to be a profitable trade, and many a captain who has failed to get a freight of any other description has done a good thing in pilgrims for his owners. They are usually taken as deck passengers, paying from two pounds to four pounds a piece for the voyage. In return for this, the captain finds them only with fresh water and fuel. They bring their own provisions, principally of a vegetable kind. Few things are more picturesque than to see a group of these wanderers on the deck of a steamer. Each squats in the particular corner which he may have appropriated, and wrapped in his white *bernouse* seems sublimely indifferent to all that goes on. As the setting sun begins to send its last red rays over the scene, the pious pilgrim may be seen to rise from his post and place himself with his face towards Mecca; he first stands erect in silent prayer, he next falls on his knees and bows his head to the ground several times. His devotions ended, he unfolds his blankets, which, like Joseph's coat, are of many colours, and subsides into slumber. As a rule, the pilgrims make quiet and contented passengers. When roused, however, by injustice or ill-treatment, they have been known to give a great deal of trouble. In the few instances in which this has occurred they have had abundant reason. Not more than a year or two ago, a firm on the shores of the Red Sea, of which, I am sorry to say, some of the members were of English nationality, gave passage tickets to several hundred pilgrims who desired to be conveyed to Tunis. On arrival at Suez the passengers accidentally discovered that the vessel would be sent to a totally different port. Naturally indignant, they demanded a return of their passage money. This was refused and the rest was that the Agent's office was mobbed, and himself threatened with violence. Eventually they were persuaded to go to Alexandria, and lay their case before the International Tribunals. The sight of some four hundred of these poor men crouching on the steps of the Palais de Justice will not soon be forgotten. In the end, I am happy to say that they had justice done them so far as was possible, the Court ordering the shipowners to refund a portion of the passage money, and to forward the pilgrims to their homes. This relief came none too soon, for the men were in a simply destitute condition, and the Egyptian Government was forced to provide them with food and shelter in the meantime. Besides frauds of this kind, pilgrims are exposed to other dangers. It is not many years since some hundreds of them were washed overboard from the deck of an Austrian Lloyd steamer in the Levant, and other cases could, if necessary, be cited. The regulation is that not more than three pilgrims should be carried for every two tons of the ship's measurement, but it is by no means generally observed, and instances of overcrowding are rather the rule than the exception. Occasionally, too, an epidemic, like cholera or smallpox, breaks out on board, and the pilgrims, huddled together, badly fed, and ill cared for, die off in great numbers.

Cape Guardafui, where the *Jeddah* was deserted by her Captain, is situated at the easternmost point of Africa, in latitude 11.49 North and longitude 51.20 East, and has proved fatal to many a vessel. It is a bold, prominent headland leading up to the Straits of Bab-el-Mandeb, at the entrance to the Red Sea. The words Bab-el-Mandeb signify "The Gate of

Tears," and the name was given to the spot by the early navigators to show their sense of the perils attending its navigation. The currents off Cape Guardafui run very strong, and vary in direction according to the state of the wind. These, however, would not be the principal danger which a vessel on a voyage like that of the *Jeddah* would have to contend with. At this season of the year the south-west monsoon is blowing in all its strength. The effect of this is to produce most violent sand-storms. During the prevalence of one of these not only is the sky obscured for several miles out to sea, but dust and sand fall on a ship's deck in quantities that would seem incredible. As a natural consequence all distant objects become invisible even at noonday. The probability is that during a storm of this character the *Jeddah* ran upon one of the reefs of coral and lava immediately off Guardafui, without ever seeing the Cape itself. To show how likely such an event may be, it may be mentioned that the steamship *Garonne*, belonging to the Orient Line, not many months ago passed thirty-one hours on a reef immediately under Cape Guardafui, without once seeing that promontory. The Messageries steam-ship *Meikong*, and a Dutch steamer, the *Oberyssel*, also figured amongst those which have lately come to grief at the same place.

The subject of erecting a lighthouse on Cape Guardafui, or on the neighbouring Cape Ras-Hafun, has been much agitated lately, and a slight increase on the dues of vessels passing the Suez Canal to meet the expense is talked of. The difficulties in the way, however, are twofold. In the first place, Guardafui is situated in a wild, lawless country, and it would, in the event of a lighthouse being resolved upon, be necessary to establish a fortification, with a garrison to protect it. In the next place, in the opinion of navigators, a lighthouse in such a position would only be an additional element of danger, in tempting ships to take a course which they should always avoid. Every one knows how much the utility of a lighthouse is impaired by an ordinary sea fog: *à fortiori*, in a sandstorm, such as accompanies the monsoon it would be invisible altogether. Cape Guardafui is situated to the west-south-west of the Island of Socotra, whose granite hills, five thousand feet in height, form a landmark which can hardly be mistaken. By steering along the north side of Socotra a safe and easy channel is found; by going on the south side a saving of about twenty miles may be effected. This, however, in a place where the current has been known to set a vessel sixty miles out of her course in twenty-four hours, and where the land is obscured by perpetual sandstorms, is accompanied by risks which no prudent navigator would care to incur. It may be positively affirmed that as long as ships persist in passing to the south side of Socotra during the southwest monsoon they incur risks from which no lighthouse can protect them.

From *The Daily Times*, 11 September.

THE JEDDAH INCIDENT AND THE LONDON PAPERS.

THE telegram announcing the supposed loss of the steamer *Jeddah* with 1,000 souls on board appears to have created nearly as great [a] sensation in London on the morning the 11th August as the *Kandahar* disaster and excited quite a thrill of horror, a feeling which was succeeded by quite a different one when later news was received that the steamer had been towed safely into Aden with all her hapless passengers, and that she had simply been abandoned, prematurely, by the Captain and Officers. Captain Clark's statement as to the circumstances under which he abandoned his ship, which we published the other day, can only be characterised as a most perfunctory and unsatisfactory one, which explains nothing and which certainly furnishes no defence to the strongly general adverse opinion as to his conduct. We had hoped to have full details in the Indians [*sic*] papers about the subject, but nothing appears in any of them except the following paragraph from the *Times of India* of the 24th August:

Our Aden correspondent writes under date August 10:

"I have just heard that a vessel belonging to the Singapore Steam Ship Company, named *Jeddah*, has been lost off the north end of Socotra, with over 900 pilgrims on board. The captain (Clark), his wife, chief mate, chief engineer, and two others, and sixteen natives arrived here just now in the S.S. *Scindia*. The *Jeddah* was pitching about in a heavy sea and her boilers started from their fastenings, and took charge of the engine room, and, as you may imagine, soon knocked a hole in the ship's side. The pilgrims murdered the second officer and second engineer, and did their best to kill the Europeans who have been saved, by throwing boxes and other heavy articles into the boat as she was being launched. The captain's wife was passed out of the sinking ship through one of the ports. When the boat shoved off the *Jeddah* was sinking fast. I am told that it was an awful business, but I have no time to send further particulars by this mail."

We now learn that on the 12th, the *Jeddah*, much to the astonishment of Captain Clark, was towed into Aden harbour with all the passengers on board. Pending the result of the inquiry into the matter that Government will of course order, the public will do well to suspend their judgement, and not to censure Captain Clark for what at first sight does look very like a heartless desertion of his ship. It may prove that he was driven to take his wife off by the conduct of the pilgrims, who, if our correspondent is correctly informed, not only murdered one of the officers of the vessel and an engineer, but did their best to kill the other Europeans also.

The London papers of the 12th August nearly all comment upon the abandonment of the steamer, as will be seen by the following extracts:

(Times.)

London was startled yesterday by the announcement of a disaster which, if true, would have been the most dreadful of recent times. The news was that a ship named the *Jeddah*, of Singapore, bound for Jeddah, had foundered last Sunday off Cape Guardafui, the easternmost point of Africa, near the Straits of Rab-el-Mandeb, with 935 Mohammedan pilgrims on board. All, it was stated, had perished, excepting the captain, his wife, the chief engineer, the assistant engineer, and sixteen natives. The survivors had been picked up by the steamer *Scindia* and landed at Aden. There was something very unpleasant in the facts thus stated; for, to honour of sailors, nothing is more rare than that, in a disaster at sea, the captain and the principal officers of the vessel should be the chief or sole survivors. Nothing can be more admirable than the manner in which, as a rule, the commanders of vessels stay by them to the end, and insist on being the last rather than the first to be saved. Apart from this consideration, the reported loss of life was unprecedented in such an accident, and would have amounted to more than the average total loss on British vessels during the year. But before we have had time to realise the extent of the disaster, the still stranger news arrives that it has never occurred. A telegram from Aden states that the vessel arrived there yesterday in tow of another steamer. She had been abandoned at sea, but did not founder as the master had reported. This statement is an immense relief; but as need hardly be urged, it suggests inquiries of a very painful character. Was the vessel, with this vast number of passengers on board, actually abandoned by the master and some of his chief officers? If she was towed into Aden, she could not have been in a condition which would justify her officers in leaving her at all; and the abandonment of duty which would be involved in such conduct is so disgraceful that we must regard the whole matter as a mystery until full particulars are furnished. It would have been terrible that more than nine hundred helpless pilgrims should have perished at sea. But that they should have been abandoned by officers of the ship to which they had intrusted themselves, and saved by the accidental services rendered them by another vessel, is scarcely credible.

(Daily News.)

Yesterday the public was startled by the report, very positively affirmed, of the foundering of the steamer *Jeddah*, off Cape Guardafui. The vessel, which was said to have been lost, was bound from Singapore to the port from which she took her name with pilgrims for Mecca. She carried, it is said, 953 pilgrims, and all on board were described as having perished, except the captain, his wife, the first officer, the two principal engineers, and sixteen "natives," whether passengers or Lascar sailors was not stated. If the story had been true, 931 souls must have perished, a number which has, perhaps, never been equalled in the loss of a single ship, save occasionally in the old days of heavily-manned sailing first-rates. But the story is not true. The survivors, as they were deemed, were picked up by an English steamer, and landed at Aden, and they told the tale now happily contradicted. The captain and his wife, together with his principal officers, appear to have deserted the vessel under the impression that she was about to founder, and to have reported to their rescuers that she had foundered. Happily the fears on which they had acted were not confirmed by the result. The *Jeddah* arrived at Aden all safe a few hours after she had been left to what seemed an inevitable fate, towed by the steamer *Antenor*. The relief which is felt at the safety of the pilgrims will be modified by a feeling of indignation and horror at what seems the cowardly desertion of their post and trust by the master and seamen of the ship. They may be able, though we do not see how, to acquit themselves of a poltroonery rarer among sailors than the calamity would have been, which they seem to have shunned for themselves and left to their passengers.

(Daily Chronicle.)

THE alarming announcement made yesterday in a Reuter's telegram from Aden to the effect that the steamship *Jeddah*, of Singapore, had foundered off Cape Guardafui with a thousand passengers on board has fortunately turned out to be incorrect. The first telegram, which appeared in our second edition yesterday, stated that all on board the vessel had perished excepting the captain, his wife, the chief officer, the chief engineer, the assistant engineer, and sixteen "natives" – probably members of the crew. After abandoning the ship, they were picked up by the steamer *Scindia* and landed at Aden, where the captain reported that his vessel had gone down on the 8th instant. Her passengers, about a thousand in number, consisted of pilgrims on their way to Mecca. At the time the captain left the ship she was within two days' sail of Jeddah, the nearest port to Mecca. That she should thus have been abandoned and her living freight left to their fate is one of the most dastardly circumstances we have ever heard of in connection with the perils of the deep. We are assuming, of course, that the latest telegram received with reference to the affair is correct, and we see no reason to doubt it. The day after the *Scindia* had landed the runaway captain of the *Jeddah* and his companions at Aden, the abandoned ship was towed into the same port by the steamship *Antenor*, which fortunately sighted her after she had been given up for lost by the very men who ought to have remained on board to the last, even had there been no hope of keeping her above water. It is to be feared that pilgrim ships are sometimes officered by unprincipled and cowardly men who disgrace the traditions of seamanship. We sincerely trust that no Englishman was amongst the boatload of cowards who left the *Jeddah* and her thousand passengers to shift for themselves. Further information as to the circumstances under which the *Antenor* fell in with the abandoned vessel and brought her safely to port would be welcome. Should the suspicions as to the conduct of the Captain of the *Jeddah* and his officers prove to be well founded, no punishment will be too severe for them. But for her good fortune in falling in with the *Antenor*, the pilgrim ship probably would have foundered sooner or later, but that the captain could have brought her safely to port, had not his own anxiety to save himself prevented him from making the effort, has been demonstrably proved.

(Globe.)

There will be a general feeling of incredulity in England as to the supposed extraordinary conduct of those officers who were in charge of the steamer *Jeddah*, abandoned off Cape Guardafui. As far as we can gather from the rather meagre accounts which have as yet been sent from Aden, it would seem that the captain of the ship and his wife, with the chief officer, the engineers, and some native seamen, left the *Jeddah* in what they supposed was a sinking condition, and made the best of their way to shore without even waiting to see whether their fears as to the safety of the vessel were justified by the event. So certain were these persons of the calamity which they anticipated, that on arriving in harbour they declared as a positive fact that the ship had foundered with all its passengers, adding, with extraordinary temerity, the intelligence that no one of them had survived to tell the tale. This news had hardly been telegraphed to England on the authority of the captain's report before a second message arrived showing that it was completely false, and that the *Jeddah*, instead of coming to a bad end, had been taken in tow by another steamer, and brought with all hands safe to Aden. It is impossible to admit without further evidence what appears at first sight to be the disgraceful behaviour of the captain and his chief officers. To abandon a ship for the purpose of saving his own life in preference to the lives of his passengers, has always been considered the extreme of cowardice and selfishness in a ship's master; and even if the *Jeddah* had afterwards foundered there would have remained an indelible stain upon the credit of the men who had thus run away at the moment of peril. But the fact that the ship was not in any extremity of peril is clearly proved by her eventual safety, and the charge becomes thus one of over-timidity as well as simple *lache*[*té*]. We do not prejudge the matter, which will have to be sifted to the bottom, but it seems possible that the nationality of the passengers, who were pilgrims from Singapore, may have led the officers to be less careful of their lives than if they had been Europeans. If this should prove to have been so, the case becomes even more discreditable, and no punishment could be too great for such an act of desertion.

There can be no doubt at all that these extracts exactly reflect what will be the general opinion as to Captain Clark's conduct all over the world, as they certainly do the local feeling here. Their severe tone of condemnation is amply and more than amply justified by the report of the Aden Court of Inquiry which we are enabled to publish to-day. The whole story is, we venture to say, unexampled in all marine history in its disgrace to the Captain and Officers of the *Jeddah*, and is calculated to remain as a slur or stain upon the whole British mercantile service, and such conduct cannot be denounced and repudiated in too strong terms.

Another matter that seems to call for some inquiry in connection with this deplorable incident is the way in which this pilgrim trade is conducted from this port. How came the *Jeddah* to have so many passengers and what provision had she for the safety of her passengers in case of accident such as actually did happen? How many boats had she, and how many boats have other steamers engaged in the same trade in comparison with the number of passengers? It seems to us that these poor helpless crowds of pilgrims have at least quite as good claims for protection from Government as the lusty Chinese coolie and his ingenuous Kling brother.

5. **Proceedings of the Legislative Council of Singapore, 14 September 1880, as recorded in the *Straits Times Overland Journal*, 20 September 1880, pp. 2-3.**

From *The Daily Times,* 16 September.

THE S.S. "JEDDAH."

OWING to the courtesy of the Colonial Secretary, we are enabled, to-day, to publish the Official Shorthand report of the proceedings in Council on Tuesday, relative to the motion brought forward by Mr. Campbell, of which a brief resume was given yesterday. The circumstances attending the abandonment of the *Jeddah* are now so prominently before the world, and

Singapore being the port in which the ship is owned and from which the pilgrims sailed the official expressions of opinion here on the conduct of the Captain and officers will naturally be considered of great importance and will be read with interest in England and elsewhere.

LEGISLATIVE COUNCIL

Tuesday. 14 September, 1880.

Present:
His Excellency The Governor.

(Sir Frederick A. Weld, K.C.M.G.)

His Honour the Chief Justice.
The Hon'ble the Colonial Secretary.
 " the Colonial Treasurer.
 " T. Shelford.
 " R. Campbell.
 " S. Gilfillan.
 " F. C. Bishop.

The Minutes of the last Meeting are read and confirmed.

The "Jeddah" Case.

Mr. Campbell: – Sir, I have given private notice to the Hon'ble the Colonial Secretary, which he has been good enough to accept, of my intention to bring before Your Excellency and this Council a matter which is creating widespread indignation among all classes of the community in Singapore, as well as in England, if we may judge from the reports received by last mail. I refer to the ruthless abandonment by her Captain of the Steamer *Jeddah* on the voyage from this port and Penang to Jeddah; and I would move:

"That in view of what has been disclosed by the Finding of the Court of Inquiry at Aden in the case of the *Jeddah*, it is the bounden duty of the local Government to adopt all the means in its power to bring the Master – Joseph Lucas Clarke [sic] – to trial, for his inhuman conduct in deserting his steamer; or, at least, to secure by representations to the Board of Trade, that his Certificate shall be suspended for such a time as will render it impossible that any lives can ever again be entrusted to his care, under the British flag."

It would appear, Sir, that this steamer left Singapore about the middle of July, and that after experiencing, as might be expected during this monsoon, heavy weather between this and Aden, on the 3rd of August it was found, when near Cape Guardafui, that her boilers had got loose, or from some reason had become detached. For four days every ordinary endeavours seem to have been made by the Captain and his Engineers to effect the necessary repairs – endeavours which seem to have been very badly conducted and imperfectly carried out – and, on the 7th of August, the Captain makes up his mind that the vessel must be abandoned; because, as he says, the Hadjis had shown the intention to murder his wife. From the evidence adduced at the Court of Inquiry, it would seem that his fears were utterly unfounded. However, he orders a boat to be lowered, in which he puts his wife and into which he, with his Chief Officer and the Chief Engineer, manage to get. That boat when being lowered is attempted to be swamped by the Hadjis – a most natural thing, I think; and I question whether any of us in the same situation would not have shot Captain Lucas Clark like a dog for his dastardly attempt to desert his vessel in such dire distress. However, he manages to get away, and on the morning of the 8th he sights the *Scindia*, and is taken on board. What does he then do? One would have thought his first impulse would be to implore the Captain of that vessel to look out for the *Jeddah*, which he must have known might have been saved. But he does not do so; he tells, as I think we may fairly assume, a deliberate falsehood, and says that the vessel had foundered; he goes on to Aden, let us hope, in a happy frame of mind, and leaves his unfortunate passengers to perish like rats in a barrel! Was anything more inhuman ever heard of? At Aden he tells a tissue of falsehoods – I have no hesitation in saying so; a Court of Inquiry is held, and the result of the inquiry is that his certificate is suspended for three years. During the inquiry not one extenuating circumstance was brought forward, and not one single excuse could be shown for the Captain's conduct. He seems all through to have acted in a most inhuman and dastardly manner; and what is the result? Merely that his certificate is suspended for three years!

Now, Sir, I hold that that is a punishment quite inadequate for the misdemeanour he has committed. Why, the man is a murderer. He was instrumental in causing the death of his Second Mate and the others who perished with him, and he put in jeopardy the lives of over 900 pilgrims, thus casting disgrace upon the British Mercantile Marine, of which he has been an unworthy member, and a slur upon the British flag.

What I desire to urge is that the local Government here should take any steps in its power to intensify the punishment of Clark by a criminal prosecution, or at any rate to perpetuate his disgrace by representing his conduct to the Board of Trade in such a manner that that Body may take care that his certificate be never again renewed. It may be argued that the Government here has no jurisdiction. That I question very much. At any rate, the Government is bound to protect the pilgrim traffic from these ports, and to show these devotees, and others in this Colony, that such unprincipled conduct as Clark's does not pass unheeded. I find that the law lays down very clearly how the Government may interfere with merchant seamen who misconduct themselves. It says: "Any master of, or any seaman or apprentice belonging to any British ship who by wilful breach of duty, or by neglect of duty, or by reason of drunkenness, does any act tending to the immediate loss, destruction, or serious damage of such ship, or tending immediately to endanger the life or limb of any person belonging to or on board of such ship, or why by wilful breach of duty, or by neglect of duty, or by reasons of drunkenness refuses or omits to do any lawful act, proper and requisite to be done by him for preserving such ship from immediate loss, destruction, or serious damage, or for preserving any person belonging to or on board of such ship from immediate danger to life or limb, shall for every such offence be deemed guilty of a misdemeanour."

The punishment for such misdemeanours is laid down: "Every offence by this Act declared to be a misdemeanour shall be punishable by fine or imprisonment with or without hard labour."

And then.

"For the purpose of giving jurisdiction under this Act, every offence shall be deemed to have been committed, and every cause of complaint to have arisen, either in the place in which the same actually was committed or arose, or in any place in which the offender or person complained against may be."

It seems to me, therefore, that the Merchant Shipping Act extends to all parts of Her Majesty's dominions and colonies and that Clark can be prosecuted under that Act for the serious and grave misdemeanour he has committed. The Court of Inquiry at Aden was simply a Court of Inquiry. It may be argued that the Government in India can, and will probably, deal with the case, but I trust the local Government here will take the initiative, and show the people at home, what they no doubt will expect, that we are equal to the occasion and will act accordingly.

Mr. GILFILLAN: – Sir, I rise to second the motion which has been made by the Hon'ble member opposite. When any fair-minded man reads the particulars of such an incident as is set forth in the Finding of this Court of Inquiry, his first impulse naturally is to discover, if possible, some ground of arrest of the execration that is naturally felt for the man who could have been guilty of such an act. I have gone carefully through these papers with this purpose, and I can find no circumstance which tends to qualify the feeling of horror that is excited at what was done by Captain Clark. The facts seem very simple: that the ship being, in the opinion of the Captain, in danger of sinking, he proceeded to get out the boats, not with the intention of caring for the lives of those who had to look to him, and to no one else, for their protection under these circumstances – whom he was bound as much by duty as by feelings of common humanity to make his first consideration, – but simply to provide for his wife – which might be natural enough, if he had remembered that other people on board his sinking ship had wives as well as himself – and to make sure of the preservation of his own valuable life. Not only does he thus disgracefully desert the ship and passengers, but next morning, when one would think he had had time to reflect – time for his heart to be touched with pity for these thousand souls whom he had left to sink helplessly – when he himself is picked up, he apparently gives not one thought to these poor creatures whom he had so cruelly deserted, nor does he so far as we can learn, suggest to the Captain of the *Scindia* that he should put about and see even if any chance survivor should be floating upon some fragment of wreck, but goes contentedly on to Aden. Coming back here, there is published in his name, what I believe is authentic, a statement in the papers which is intended evidently as a sort of justification of his action. In this he says that one of the reasons of his leaving the ship was that his wife's life had been threatened by the passengers. This allegation is specially dealt with by the Court of Inquiry, and according to their report there is no truth in it. There was no talk of threats until such time as these passengers found they were being deserted by the man of all others who was bound to protect and care for them. He further states that, when he was trying to get away from the ship and leave his passengers to their fate, things – boxes and what not – were thrown at him. Very unaccountable to his mind! Sir, I think if those 900 passengers had been English, he would not have been so leniently treated. There is a rough manner of dealing with cases of this kind, not unknown among men of our race, and if he had found himself getting a quick run by a line to the yard-arm, I do not think any one who has studied the circumstances would say he was harshly dealt with.

Our business, Sir, is not so much to take exception to the Finding of the Court of Inquiry, however much we may feel that it errs on the side of leniency: this will, no doubt, be revised in the proper quarter, but it at all events lies with us to express the feeling of reprobation which this deed inspires, and to do what in us lies, with the assistance of the Government, to secure that a man so unhappily constituted as Captain Clark seems to be shall not, on any future occasion, have the opportunity of having passengers put under his care or trusted to his humanity. I beg to second the resolution proposed by my Hon'ble friend.

The COLONIAL SECRETARY: – It would have been surprising, Sir, if an occurrence of this kind had not engaged the attention of this Council. The ship sailed from the waters of this Colony, under the laws and other requirements of this Colony, and naturally, therefore, it behoved this Government to do what it could towards seeing that the law is observed. There is, I need hardly point out to those who look at the question, an exceeding difficulty for the Government at this time to take action. We are not in possession, up to the present hour, of any official record of the proceedings of the Court of Inquiry. Not only is this important and indispensable document wanting to us, but we are not in receipt of the evidence taken at the Court of Inquiry. Had that evidence, however, been in our possession, it might have been possible for the Government to take action. I say only "might have been possible," because at the present time there is not one single person in the Colony who could give evidence for the Crown against the accused person, or the person who ought to be accused. Consequently, in dealing with this case as a criminal matter, I think it would be a very indiscreet thing for the Government to initiate proceedings, without the means to proceed to a proper termination. That there is sufficient power under the Merchant Shipping Act for the Government to prosecute Joseph Lucas Clark for his conduct in connection with the case of the *Jeddah* is beyond doubt, but to take such proceedings it is necessary there should be a clear and unquestionable amount of evidence to support the charge. If it comes within the knowledge of the Government that it is possible to institute criminal proceedings against Clark, I can assure my Hon'ble friends that the Government will look upon it as a most important duty to do so; but, as at present advised, there is not sufficient to justify any such action on the part of the Government. It will, however, be satisfactory to the Council to know that, as far as the *Jeddah* is concerned, she left this port after having been in dry dock and been most carefully overhauled, and before she sailed, every requirement which the law imposes upon owners and masters was attended to by the authorities of the port.

The case has created excitement not only in our own minds, but of course has affected the whole character of English seamanship throughout the world. I do not think that any one could read the account without the blood mantling to his cheeks with shame. Our character stands deservedly high for seamanship, not only as regards Her Majesty's Navy, but also as regards the Mercantile Marine of the United Kingdom; and when a case like this occurs, of such gross cowardice on the part of a man who is placed in charge of a number of miserable pilgrims unable to protect themselves in such circumstances, no punishment the law could impose would be too much for such a criminal. But the case is one which is, as far as I can see at present, beyond the power of Government to deal with it. There have been proceedings before a competent Court of Inquiry, and that Court, in the exercise of its powers, has not thought proper to send the case of the Master before a Magistrate in order that it might be investigated. Why it has not done so is not for me to say. It is incredible that a Court coming to such a decision as is set out in the Finding could think it was a sufficient punishment to suspend the Master's certificate for three years. However, under the law, – I speak subject to correction, – the Board of Trade has supreme authority to amend the decision of the Court of Inquiry: If the punishment is too severe, it can modify it; and if it is too light, it can increase it; and for myself, I have very little doubt that, when this case comes under the cognizance of the Board of Trade, as it must do under the

Merchant Shipping Act, the Board of Trade will impose, according to its powers, the severest punishment on Captain Clark that the law will admit.

The GOVERNOR. – I had not intended to speak on this subject, but I wish to say a word or two on what has passed. Hon'ble gentlemen may be sure that I yield to no one in my detestation of the conduct, if it be such as has been represented, not only on the part of Captain Clark, whose name alone has been mentioned, but also on the part of some, indeed apparently nearly all of his officers, which does indeed reflect disgrace upon the Mercantile Navy, whose commanders have generally behaved so well and reflected such credit upon our nation in cases of that kind. But the Council must remember that if the Government took hasty proceedings, instead of acting to the detriment of those whose conduct is now impugned it would be an advantage to them, because if that prosecution failed in consequence of insufficient evidence, it would really militate in their favour when the case came before the Board of Trade, because they would plead acquittal. Now I quite concur with what has been said, as far as I know the case, – and I simply know it, as all of us do, through the newspaper accounts, and from the very lame defence, as it seemed to me, of Captain Clark. Therefore I concur with the views expressed by the members of Council to-day: and one thing I would say, that whether we find it possible to take legal proceedings or not, the Council may be assured that I shall bring the case under the notice of the Secretary of State prominently by a despatch, and that I shall be fortified in so doing by the expressions of members of the Council, which, I am sure I may say without fear of contradiction, are concurred in by every member who sits around this table.

Mr. GILFILLAN: – May I be allowed one word by way of explanation? In addressing the Council just now, I omitted to call the attention of the Government to two points in the report of the Court of Inquiry which seem specially to call for their consideration. One is the statement that the number of boats provided was insufficient to accommodate more than about one-fourth of the people on board; and the other is the opinion expressed that the number of passengers taken was too many for a ship of the size of the *Jeddah*.

The COLONIAL SECRETARY: – This matter has not been overlooked, but, as a matter of fact, I have it from the Master Attendant that the ship left this port with all the requirements of the law observed. I believe, from what I have heard, that a ship carrying passengers very rarely carries sufficient boats for all the passengers, but, as a matter of fact, the *Jeddah* carried all the boat accommodation required by law, and of course the local Government could not require her to have more than the law allowed.

Mr. SHELFORD: – I may add to that, the *Jeddah* brought a certificate from home to carry 960 troops, and of course her boats would not have been sufficient for that number.

Mr. CAMPBELL: – I think, after the very satisfactory assurances from Your Excellency and from the Colonial Secretary, there is nothing left for me but to withdraw the motion I have made.

The GOVERNOR: – Yes, I think all your objects have been attained. The motion is withdrawn.

6. **Report on the Action for Salvage brought against the *Jeddah* in the Vice Admiralty Court of the Straits Settlements, from the *Straits Times Overland Journal*, 22 October 1881, pp. 3-4.**

From *The Daily Times*, 20 October.

IN THE VICE ADMIRALTY COURT OF THE STRAITS SETTLEMENTS.

MONDAY, 17TH OCTOBER, 1881.
BEFORE SIR THOMAS SEDGREAVES, KT. CHIEF JUSTICE.

In the matter of
The British Steamship *Jeddah*,
J. L. Clark, Master.

JUDGEMENT.

This was an action for salvage brought by Alfred Holt, managing partner of the Ocean Steam Ship Company of Liverpool, owners of the British steamship *Antenor* of Liverpool, on behalf of the owners, masters and crew of the said steamship *Antenor*, against the steamship *Jeddah*, her cargo and freight.

Mr. Donaldson and Mr. Burkinshaw, appeared on behalf of the Plaintiffs.

Mr. Davidson on behalf of the Defendants.

The case was tried before the Court on the 12th, 13th, 14th, 15th, 16th, and 17th September.

The *Jeddah* is a British steamship belonging to the Singapore Steamship Company Limited, of the burthen of 993 tons or thereabouts. She sailed from Singapore on the 17th July 1880, on a voyage to Jeddah, arrived at Penang on the 19th, and left on the following day with a general cargo and 953 passengers bound for Jeddah. What happened to her afterwards is then described by Captain Clarke [*sic*], the Master, in the Protest subsequently made by him on the 26th November, 1880.

"During the twenty-fifth, twenty-sixth, and twenty-seventh, the vessel encountered heavy squalls of wind and rain at intervals with very heavy Northwest swell, causing her to roll and labour very severely, breaking everything about the decks and filling the cabins with water. All hands were constantly employed baling out water during the twenty-seventh, and on that day some of the water-closet pipes started, causing a quantity of water to come into the saloon, and towards midnight and during the next day, the twenty-eighth, the weather cleared up and the sea decreased. At noon on the second August, there was a moderate gale and rising sea, causing the engines to race and the vessel to pitch badly and shipping much water forward, and the vessel being in latitude five degrees thirty minutes North, and longitude sixty one degrees six minutes East at noon on that day. At 7.0 p.m. the foretopmast staysail was blown away, and the water from the broken closet pipe continued to come into the fore and after cabins, as the leaks could not be got at. During the third August the wind blew a very strong gale and a fearful sea was running, washing the decks clear fore and aft of two native water-closets and all moveables, and causing a heavy strain on the engines and boilers. The same and even worse weather continued on the fifth, and it became necessary to stop the fresh water condenser to enable the donkey engine to pump the bilges, the water in which was increasing more than the main pumps could reduce. On the sixth August, the weather still the same, the vessel, engines and boilers straining so severely that at 9 20 a.m. the first engineer reported that the donkey feed check valve-chest on port boiler had broken in two just above the valve-seat, owing to the boilers shifting with the rolling of the vessel. This necessitated drawing the fires in the port boiler, to put an India rubber washer over valve-seat. When this had been done, the starboard valve-chest gave way in the same manner, and the fires in the starboard boiler were drawn and steam got up in the port boiler. During the repairs, the water in the bilges had increased from about eighteen inches to twenty four inches, and on starting the engines, the chief engineer ordered the bilge injection to be opened; this reduced the water to about fourteen inches, when the bilge injection got choked, and while it was being cleared, on the morning of the seventh August, the main feed pipe of the port boiler gave way in the same place as the other pipes had done, and shortly afterwards the steam pipe from the donkey boiler connected to the superheater broke in two from the straining and shifting of the boilers. The wooden shores that had been placed during the voyage to prevent the boilers shifting were washed away by the water in the vessel. At 7 a.m. on the same day, the seventh August, it was still blowing a tremendous gale, and the water in the vessel rose above the fire grates, the boilers started adrift from their seatings, and the stokehole and engine-room plates and bearers dashed about with every roll of the vessel. It now seemed that the vessel had sprung a heavy leak, and as nothing more could be done in the engine room or stokehole and the water was rising so rapidly, every deck pump was set to work and the firemen and passengers employed day and night at the pumps and baling water with buckets. Sails were also passed under the bottom of the vessel, but the water still increased a foot in twelve hours. An attempt was now made to disconnect the propeller, but the water was rising so rapidly, and was already at such a dangerous height, it was found impossible to do so. While it was safe, the sea cocks were examined and found to be properly closed. At midnight on the seventh to eighth the passengers refused to pump any more, and the vessel settled down by the stern with a heavy list to starboard, and at 2 a.m. this appearer [i.e. Captain Clark] left the vessel in one of the ship's boats and arrived at Aden on the tenth of August." At the same time the *Jeddah* was abandoned by all her officers and crew, except the 2nd Engineer, who was ignorant of navigation, the Serang, Supercargo and Clerk, 4 klassies and 13 firemen.

On the 8th August, at 5 p.m. the *Antenor*, an iron screw steamship of 1,644 tons, bound on a voyage from Shanghai to London, and with a full complement of 680 passengers, sighted a vessel which subsequently proved to be the *Jeddah*, flying signals of distress. The signals of distress were, on one mast, "We are sinking;" on another, "Send immediate assistance." The flying of the first signal was denied by the Defendants' reply, but was clearly proved not only by the witnesses called on behalf of the Plaintiffs, but by one of the witnesses, Mahomed Khan, clerk on board the

Jeddah, called by the Defendants. A boat containing the first mate, the boatswain, and four of the crew of the *Antenor*, was sent, and on boarding her they found the *Jeddah* in a very disabled condition. According to the Act on Petition framed upon the affidavits of the Captain and Chief Officer of the *Antenor*, "the Engines were totally disabled, and the Engine fires put out; there were 7 or 8 feet of water in the vessel, and everything on board was in confusion, and all persons on board were panic stricken until the arrival on board of the First Mate and Boatswain of the *Antenor*. The boilers on board were adrift and had broken from their fastenings, and all the pipe connections with the boilers were broken, and no steam power on board could be used. The steam pipes on board could not be used, and all fires were out. The position was about 13 miles to the westward of Cape Guardafui and about 9 miles from the African coast. She was under foretopsail jib, and fore and main topsails, and was heading for some bluffs 1,300 feet high on the Coast of Africa. There was an East wind blowing, with a heavy ground swell, and the vessel was being driven through the water in a quasi-derelict condition at the rate of 2½ to 3 knots an hour toward the coast. A heavy surf was breaking on the coast, and it was becoming rapidly dark as the sun set at 6 p.m." After the Chief Mate had ascertained by personal observation the state of things on board the *Jeddah*, he returned to the *Antenor* and reported to the Captain. It must be admitted that the Captain found himself confronted with a task of no ordinary difficulty. In command of a ship with a valuable cargo and a full complement of passengers on board, whose interests and those of his owners he was first bound to consider, and with darkness fast coming on, he had to choose between jeopardizing his own ship, cargo and passengers, or leaving a ship abandoned by the Captain and officers, and with nearly 1,000 souls on board, to the inevitable fate that seemed to await her of foundering at sea or being dashed to pieces on the coast. After a short consultation between the Captain and the Chief Officer it was decided to make an attempt to save the *Jeddah*. They considered it impossible to take the *Jeddah*'s passengers on board the *Antenor*, as "the *Antenor*" was already full, but they thought that it might be possible to tow her into Aden if they could manage to keep her afloat by inducing the pilgrims to work at the pumps. The Chief Officer returned to the *Jeddah* with the Boatswain and 4 of the crew, after arranging signals with the Captain to be used in case of the *Jeddah* sinking, so as to take them off in time. The boatswain and crew returned to the *Antenor* at 10 p.m. but from that time until the

Jeddah was successfully towed into Aden, the Chief Officer never left her. Though taking the *Jeddah* in tow was accomplished after considerable difficulty, and with the exercise of much patience, skill, and ingenuity, the Chief Officer steered the *Jeddah* himself until he had taught two of the crew of the *Jeddah* to steer; and he induced the passengers to exert themselves in pumping and baling. The conclusion he had come to at first was that the ship was sinking when the *Antenor* fell in with her, and that without great exertion in baling and pumping she must sink.

He says "I called the headmen amongst the pilgrims together and organised gangs amongst the pilgrims to pump and bale the vessel. This was done, the men constantly relieving one another, and by the evening of the 9th of August, we had gained 6 inches on the water, and during the following night we gained a foot on the water and continued to gain on the water thenceforward until the water was reduced to 3½ feet in the engine room and 5 feet in the after hold." Upon this point Captain Bragg in his evidence says: "On the 9th, as the sun went half way down from the horizon, the Chief Officer telegraphed 'gained 4 inches,' and I called all hands aft to give him a cheer to encourage him – we were corresponding all the time. The question was, whether we could overpower the water, or the water overpower us. An incident of this sort, slight in itself, yet tends to shew the hearty good-will with which the sailors were conducting their operations, and how likely it would be that they would reanimate, by their coolness and determination, the failing spirits and flagging energies of the pilgrims."

Whilst the Chief Officer was thus engaged on board the *Jeddah*, the Captain and 2nd Officer of the *Antenor* kept alternate watches on board the *Antenor*, and were in constant communication with the Chief Officer by means of a board on the bridge of the *Antenor*, till, on the 11th August, at 5.15 p.m., the *Antenor*, with the *Jeddah* in tow, arrived at Aden.

On the part of the Defendants, but not until the 6th and last day of the hearing, a point which had been raised upon the pleadings was brought forward as to the jurisdiction of this Court to entertain this suit. The 19th para. of the Defendants' reply stated that "The alleged cause of action arose out of the local limits of this Court, and neither the vessel proceeded against nor any portion of the cargo or property, or effects on board thereof at the time of the said alleged salvage service, has or have come or been within the local limits of this Court since the alleged cause of action arose, and the Master of the *Jeddah* did not come within the local limits of this Court until long after this suit was commenced, wherefore the defendants say that this Court has no jurisdiction to entertain this suit."

To this the Promoters by their Rejoinder allege "That this Hon'ble Court at the commencement of this suit had and always since has had jurisdiction to entertain this suit, but that if at the commencement of this suit this Hon'ble Court had not such jurisdiction, their [sic] the Singapore Steamship Co. by their Master agreed and consented that this suit should be filed and brought in this Hon'ble Court, and that this Hon'ble Court should have jurisdiction to decide and award what amount should be paid to the Promoters in respect of the salvage services rendered to the said steamship *Jeddah*, and her cargo and passengers." The allegation in the Defendants' reply would seem to have been founded upon the 6th Sec. of the 2nd William the 4th, c.51, whereby it is enacted, "That in all cases where a ship or vessel or the Master thereof shall come within the local limits of any Vice-Admiralty Court it shall be lawful for any person to commence proceedings in any of the Suits herein before mentioned in such Vice-Admiralty Court, notwithstanding the cause of action may have arisen out of the local limits of such Court, and to carry on the same in the same manner as if the cause of action had arisen within the said limits."

The jurisdiction of the Court, however, was extended by the Vice-Admiralty Courts Act 1863, Section 13, which enacts that "The jurisdiction of the Vice-Admiralty Courts, except when it is expressly confined by this Act to matter arising within the Possession in which the Court is established, may be exercised, whether the Cause or Right of Action has arisen within or beyond the limits of such Possession." The coming within the local limits of the Vice-Admiralty Court of the ship or vessel or the Master thereof is therefore no longer necessary. The tenth Section defines the matter in respect of which the Vice-Admiralty Courts shall have jurisdiction, the 4th being "Claims in respect of salvage of any ship or of life or goods therefrom," and, as might be expected in a case of salvage, without any such words of limitation as the Act specifies. I decide, therefore, that this Court has complete jurisdiction to entertain this suit. The *Jeddah* was released at Aden, on a Bail bond being entered into in this Court on the 31st August, 1880, by five sureties, "who, submitting themselves to the jurisdiction of the Vice-Admiralty Court of the Straits Settlements, bound themselves for the said Steamship Company Limited into judgement to abide the hearing of this cause, and likewise to pay what should be adjudicated against the said steamship *Jeddah*, her cargo and freight." Although no such agreement was entered into as that contemplated by the 497th section of the Merchant Shipping Act, 1854, which taken in conjunction with section 492 allowed the salvor and Master or person in charge of the ship salved to select any Vice-Admiralty for adjudicating upon the matter, yet it would be difficult in the present case for the sureties to avoid the enforcing of their Bond, and it would be strange if the Defendants, who obtained the release of their ship on the strength of it, could now successfully decline to be bound by it. In considering the amount of salve to which the Plaintiffs are entitled, it will be convenient to consider the ingredients of salvage service under the different heads defined by the Board of Trade in Article 94 of the instructions issued by them in 1884.

    1st.   The degree of danger from which the lives or property are rescued.
    2nd.   The value of the property saved.
    3rd.   The risk incurred by the salvors.
    4th.   The value of any of the property by the use of which the services are rendered and the danger to which it is exposed.
    5th.   The skill shown in rendering the services.
    6th.   The time and labour occupied.

As regards the first of these heads, the degree of danger may be pretty correctly estimated from the actual occurrences at the time. Under what circumstances and under what impression did the captain and officers and most of the crew of the *Jeddah* abandon her at 2 a.m. on the 8th instant? The circumstances have already been set out in the Master's Report, and the inference from that is that they were leaving a sinking ship. We can infer what the condition and danger of the 953 pilgrims would be in a ship which had sprung a heavy leak and was abandoned by its Captain and officers and nearly all its crew, and had "settled down by the stern with a heavy list to starboard." At 5 p.m. on the same day, the *Antenor* is sighted by the *Jeddah*, and the signals of distress hung out by the *Jeddah* are "Send immediate assistance," "We are sinking." It is not to be wondered at that the impression under which the captain and his officers abandoned the ship to its fate at 2 a.m. still existed at 5 p.m. on the same day amongst those who could not escape from her. I cannot doubt that their then belief, however different a complexion it may have assumed a year or so afterwards, was correctly expressed by the signals, and that they did beg for immediate assistance under the belief that they were sinking. In addition to the evidence of the Captain and Officers of the *Antenor*, embodied in the Act on Petition, which shews in a strong light the dangerous position in which the *Jeddah* and the passengers on board her were in, we have the evidence of nautical men, who, by their long experience and special knowledge of the coast near which the *Jeddah* was encountered, are well qualified to form an opinion.

Captain Worsley, Master of the Telegraph ship *Sherard Osborne*, says: "I have been Master Mariner twenty years; – have commanded sailing ships and steamships in all parts of the world. I know the waters about Cape Guardafui. Under the circumstances described in the 5th and 6th paragraphs of J. T. Bragg's affidavit, I should say the *Jeddah* was in great danger. If the *Antenor* had not come up to her, I believe she would have become a total wreck. It would not have been practicable to put her about unless they got the propeller to revolve, i.e., disconnected the propeller; it is not usual to have special disconnecting gear on such ships. She was heading right on to shore, I don't think she could have been steered so as to land on any particular spot on the beach. I should have considered her a hopeless derelict, – worse than a derelict with all those people on board. I don't think she could have been, under the circumstances, brought up under her anchor, if they had let the anchor go. If she had a steam windlass on board I think she would have run an awful risk for fear of the chain carrying away the bows. If it were blowing a gale outside, there would be a heavy ground swell off Cape Guardafui – there would be surf on the shore. I don't think boats would have lived through the surf. I don't know the nature of the bottom – if coral it would be very bad holding. I think that when a ship was left as she was described to be, she was in a helpless state. Second Engineers in ships of this class do not know about the navigation of a ship. The Carpenter is the important man under the Chief Officer as regards anchoring. After hearing the accounts read on the affidavits of Bragg and Campbell of how the *Antenor* got the *Jeddah* off in that night, I think the *Antenor* ran considerable risk; even in smooth water there is risk of collision in a large steamer going alongside another near enough to take a hawser on board, more particularly when there is a strong current running, as there is there. The darkness would enhance the risk. There was very serious risk to the *Antenor*'s screw, so great that unless there was imminent danger I should not attempt it until daylight. If the *Antenor* had snapped her rope and fouled her screw she would have been in danger."

Charles Powell, in his evidence, stated: "Last year I was in command of the *Lusitania*, one of the Orient line, of nearly 4,000 tons. I passed Cape Guardafui on August 7th at noon. We had very stiff weather from Ras Hafun to Guardafui; after we got round Guardafui there was a stiff breeze to the next point to East, I know this coast pretty well. Having heard the position and circumstances of the *Jeddah*, with the native crew and great part of them gone, and with 900 and odd pilgrims on board, I consider she was in great danger. If the *Antenor* had not come up to the *Jeddah*, I certainly think at night-time she would have gone on shore. She was heading for the bluffs. If I had been on board as a passenger I should have considered her case as a very hopeless one. I consider she was in great danger when first sighted, having so much water in her hold; she could not be steered at all. From Mr. Campbell's description, I should say it was blowing a strong breeze; it corresponds with my experience of the day: this was at the height of the monsoon when a strong breeze is generally blowing. If she made any speed at all it must have been with the help of her canvas; when she was picked up I think she was waterlogged. I think she would have gone ashore before daylight. If they had succeeded in getting the anchor down, it was just a chance if they held on: there was danger to the *Antenor* of colliding, and also of getting the hawser foul of her screw – a real danger. If I had been in command of the *Antenor*, I should have considered the position a dangerous one as regards the *Antenor*, and a very risky thing to do."

There can be no doubt, I think, that the *Jeddah* was in imminent danger when she was sighted by the *Antenor*, and that but for the services rendered her by the *Antenor* she would in all probability have foundered or been dashed to pieces with the loss of every life on board. Taking into consideration the number of the lives thus rescued from the probability of impending death, this is I believe a case of life-salvage of a totally unprecedented character. As regards the value of the property salved, it appears that the *Jeddah* was insured for £30,000. Mr. Fittock, Lloyds' and Marine Surveyor, says that he valued the *Jeddah* before she went on her last voyage in dry dock at Tanjong Pagar, and that he valued her, with her stores and equipments, exclusive of coals, at £20,000. Mr. Thyne, the Port Officer at Aden, in his evidence taken on Commission at Aden, says, "My idea of the value of the *Jeddah* when she arrived at Aden is that she was worth between £14,000 and £17,000." This is rather a vague estimate, and it does not appear that he examined her in the same manner that Mr.

Fittock did at Singapore. I estimate the value of the *Jeddah* at the time that she was salved by the *Antenor* at £19,000, her cargo at about £5,000, specie on board £55, coals £300, freight for goods about £500, freight for passengers £4,025: – the result of those figures will be £28,880, or in round numbers the value of the *Jeddah*, her cargo and freight, may be put at £29,000.

The value of the cargo salved was sought to be enhanced by a claim for £27,656 in respect of money or specie and goods belonging to the passengers. There was no distinct evidence upon this point, however, beyond the evidence of one man, a Boyanese, who stated that he took $170 with him, and that it just sufficed for his expenses to Mecca and back. At the hearing it was not put as a distinct claim, but that the Court might take the probability of other passengers taking money in like manner with them into consideration as enhancing the value of the services rendered. With regard to this point, after the evidence given on both sides, I have not felt myself at liberty to take this circumstance into my consideration at all.

3rd. No serious personal risk was incurred by the salvage beyond that which arose from the possibility of a collision between the two steamers and the fouling of the screw of the *Antenor* by the tow-rope.

4th. The value of the *Antenor* was £30,000, and the value of her cargo and the freight payable in respect of it was £84,000. She incurred the danger alluded to in the last paragraph, and this Mr. Powell says was a real danger; and beyond that it is claimed that she incurred risk of becoming liable to the owners of the cargo of the *Antenor* for deviation, and incurred risk of the Insurance Policies over the *Antenor* and her cargo being vitiated by reason of the *Antenor*'s deviation and the towing of the *Jeddah*. In the present state of the law upon this subject, the Court can only bear in mind and act in the spirit of the remarks made by Dr. Lushington in the case of the *True Blue* (L.R.1 P.C.255).

"We will only add that in all those cases where the Judge considers in his own mind what he ought to do with respect to the amount of salvage to be given, he can never forget that there was possibly a risk incurred by those on board the salving vessel in respect to the vacation of policies of Insurance, and in regard to actions which might be brought against the owners of the vessel by owners of cargo." It was further stated that in consequence of the operations connected with the towing of the *Jeddah* the machinery of the *Antenor* was strained and injured. Five days after leaving Aden the engines of the *Antenor* broke down through the strap of the connecting rod giving way. In the Act on Petition this is attributed to the great increased strain put upon the engines of the *Antenor* by the towing of the *Jeddah*. The costs and losses caused to the *Antenor* by the breaking down of her engines is [*sic*] estimated at £1,980. The Captain of the *Antenor* says in his affidavit, "It is not known that such breaking down was caused by the increased strain put upon the Engines of the *Antenor*, by the towing of the *Jeddah*, but such breakdown might be attributable thereto." It is impossible, therefore, to treat this damage as having been clearly caused by the salvage services, though the fact that it may have been so caused must necessarily be taken into consideration.

5. The evidence seems clearly to establish that the operation of taking the *Jeddah* in tow and carrying out the scheme of keeping her afloat till she could be towed into a place of safety was successfully completed by the constant exercise of nautical skill, as well as by unremitting care and perseverance on the part of those in charge of the *Antenor*. The expenses incurred by the *Antenor*, in connection with the salvage operations, including £100 for 2 days demurrage and £90 for coal, amounted to £253, 3s.

6. The time occupied was as nearly as possible 3 days, and there was a further delay of 6½ hours at Aden. The labour involved was constant and severe for the first 5 hours; after that, great care and patience and perseverance were required and exercised.

The principal feature in this case is undoubtedly the life salvage, and by the Merchant Shipping Act the preservation of human life is made a distinct ground of salvage reward, with priority over all other claims for salvage where the property is insufficient. The value of the property salved is large, and it was undoubtedly salved when in imminent peril, although fortunately without any very great risk to the lives of the salvors. The employment of the *Antenor* and her valuable cargo on board upon the operation was clearly a service of very high merit, and as such ought to be liberally rewarded. I award as salvage the sum of £6000, – £4000 to go to the Owners of the *Antenor*, this sum to cover all expenses incurred by that ship – and £2000 to the Captain, Officers, and crew of the *Antenor*. Having been asked to apportion this sum, I do so as follows. The Captain and Chief Mate £500 each. The Chief Engineer and 2nd Officer £150 each; the balance to be divided amongst the remaining officers and crew according to their respective ratings, the Boatswain and 4 of the crew who went on two occasions to the *Jeddah* on the night of 8th August taking at the rate of 2 shares each.

JOPI NYMAN

Under English Eyes: Constructions of Europe in Early Twentieth-Century British Fiction

Amsterdam/Atlanta, GA 2000. VII,211 pp.
(Costerus NS 129)
ISBN: 90-420-1572-1   Hfl. 80,-/US-$ 34.-

British fictions of the early twentieth century appear obsessed with Europe. Various texts from E.M. Forster and D.H. Lawrence to Bram Stoker and the period's travel writing explore European spaces, constructing the European as an Other threatening the position of the English. What they constantly repeat is England's difference and the secondary role of European spaces, whose representation resembles that of colonial lands. By reading selected texts, both canonized and popular, published between 1894 and 1916, this study argues that this xenophobic construction is a sign of the pervading presence of concerns related to the maintenance of English national identity, Englishness, allegedly threatened by the European Other. By drawing on current postcolonial theory, the case studies in the volume show that the discourse on the Other produced in British writings on Europe contributes more than has been understood to the making and promoting of Englishness. The authors studied include D.H. Lawrence, Katherine Mansfield, Anthony Hope, Arnold Bennett, Mrs Alec Tweedie, Erskine Childers, and Joseph Conrad. The study will renew our understanding of the role of Europe in the period's cultural imagination, showing that the identities of the English are formed in encounters with different internal and external Others.

Editions Rodopi B.V.

USA/Canada: 6075 Roswell Rd., Ste. 219, Atlanta, GA 30328, Tel. (404) 843-4445, *Call toll-free* (U.S.only) 1-800-225-3998, Fax (404) 843-4315

All Other Countries: Tijnmuiden 7, 1046 AK Amsterdam, The Netherlands. Tel. ++ 31 (0)20 6114821, Fax ++ 31 (0)20 4472979
  orders-queries@rodopi.nl ----- http://www.rodopi.nl

TRICKS WITH A GLASS
Writing Ethnicity in Canada

Ed. by Rocío G. Davis & Rosalía Baena

Amsterdam/Atlanta, GA 2000. XXIV,301 pp.
(Cross/Cultures 46)
ISBN: 90-420-1213-7   Bound Hfl. 165,-/US-$ 70.-
ISBN: 90-420-1203-X   Paper Hfl. 55,-/US-$ 23.-

Studies of literary reflections on ethnicity are essential to the ever-renewed definition of Canadian literature. The essays in this collection explore the diverse ways of negotiating identity and the articulation of space in Canada, taking ethnicity as a driving force with ideological and cultural implications that lend public and literary discourse an urgent dynamism. While theorizing ethnicity is a valuable critical enterprise, these essays centre on the concrete realization of the problematics of ethnicity in creative writing, covering a wide range of Canada's mosaic. The creative inscription of ethnicity stimulates the evolution and expansion of Canada's literary heritage, the complexity of this cultural experience being the focus of the present collection. Fourteen essays, including a personal account by the Ukrainian-Canadian Janice Kulyk Keefer on the merging of private and public history, and two interviews - with the Chinese-Canadian writer Wayson Choy and the critic Linda Hutcheon - analyze the manifestations of the pluralism that has always characterized Canadian writers' consciousness of themselves, their engagement with the notion of the 'multicultural' and its significance in contemporary society and, in particular, its effect on creativity.

--------------------------   *Editions Rodopi B.V.*

USA/Canada: 6075 Roswell Rd., Ste. 219, Atlanta, GA 30328, Tel. (404) 843-4445, *Call toll-free* (U.S.only) 1-800-225-3998, Fax (404) 843-4315

All Other Countries: Tijnmuiden 7, 1046 AK Amsterdam, The Netherlands. Tel. ++ 31 (0)20 6114821, Fax ++ 31 (0)20 4472979

CEES KOSTER
From World To World. An *Armamentarium*
For the Study Of Poetic Discourse In Translation
Amsterdam/Atlanta, GA 2000. 261 pp.
(Approaches to Translation Studies 16)
ISBN: 90-420-1392-3   Hfl. 90,-/US-$ 38.-

In this book one of the old traditions of translation studies is revived: the tradition of the comparative study of translation and original. The aim of the author is to develop an *armamentarium*, a set of analytical instruments and a procedure, for the systematic study of poetic discourse in translation. The *armamentarium* provides the means to describe the 'translational interpretation', that is: the interpretation of the original as it emerges from the translation and may be constructed in the course of a comparison between the two texts.
The practical result of this study is based on a solid theoretical foundation. This study most of all reflects on the possibilities of translation comparison and description per se. It is one of the few books in which an in-depth study is undertaken into the principles of translation comparison itself, into its limits and possibilities, and into its central concepts ('shift', 'unit of comparison' etcetera). Before presenting his own proposal for a comparative procedure, the author critically evaluates several existing methods, particularly those of Toury, Van Leuven-Zwart and the German transfer-oriented approach.
The theoretical considerations in this book are amply illustrated by analyses of translated works of poets as Rutger Kopland and Robert Lowell. The book also contains an extensive case study into the translations, by the German poet Paul Celan, of a selection of William Shakespeare's sonnets.

------------------------------   *Editions Rodopi B.V.*
USA/Canada: 6075 Roswell Rd., Ste. 219, Atlanta, GA 30328, Tel. (404) 843-4314, *Call toll-free* (U.S.only) 1-800-225-3998, Fax (404) 843-4315

All Other Countries: Tijnmuiden 7, 1046 AK Amsterdam, The Netherlands. Tel. ++ **31 (0)20** 6114821, Fax ++ **31 (0)20 4472979**
orders-queries@rodopi.nl ----- http://www.rodopi.nl

A.J. SIMOES DA SILVA

The Luxury of Nationalist Despair George Lamming's Fiction as Decolonizing Project

Amsterdam/Atlanta, GA 2000. VII,219 pp.
(Cross/Cultures 44)
ISBN: 90-420-1431-8 Bound Hfl. 110,-/US-$ 47.-
ISBN: 90-420-1421-0 Paper Hfl. 40,-/US-$ 17.-

This book offers a timely critique of the work of the Barbadian novelist George Lamming, examining the ways in which his novels exhibit the "luxury of nationalist despair" and exploring the tensions between his strongly voiced anti-colonialism and his ambiguously articulated politics of self. Although stressing the place occupied by Lamming and his work in the context of an anti-colonial first generation of 'nation-writing' that has emerged in the formerly colonized world over the past half-century, the study also addresses the novelist's problematic, reductive focus on a nationalist project that is ultimately deeply flawed - in essence, the result of an uneasy relationship between form and thesis. Lamming's continued struggle with the novel as a genre, especially with its ability to get beyond the cultural and political baggage of colonialism, demonstrates the power of one of his most poignant assertions: "the colonial experience [...] is a continuing psychic experience that has to be dealt with long after the actual situation formally 'ends'."

Written from a postcolonial perspective, the study draws also on contemporary feminist criticism in order to examine Lamming's characteristically simplistic depiction of female characters in terms of a greater willingness to embody the neocolonial. The book starts by addressing the place Lamming's work occupies both within postcolonial writing at large and specifically within Caribbean literature. Subsequent chapters provide close textual readings of Lamming's six novels, paired in terms of their foregrounding of issues of race, gender and class. Despite a clear shift in Lamming's thematic focus on the rewriting of Caliban's project, with his last novel offering a basis for a re-imagining of the post/colonial encounter, there remains a perturbing inability to relinquish the privileged stance afforded the postcolonial intellectual in self-imposed exile (cultural, much more than geographical). The book represents an important contribution to criticism on the work of one of the most influential voices in postcolonial literature of the last fifty years.

Editions Rodopi B.V.

USA/Canada: 6075 Roswell Rd., Ste. 219, Atlanta, GA 30328, Tel. (404) 843-4445, *Call toll-free* (U.S.only) 1-800-225-3998, Fax (404) 843-4315

All Other Countries: Tijnmuiden 7, 1046 AK Amsterdam, The Netherlands. Tel. ++ **31 (0)20 6114821,** Fax ++ **31 (0)20**